D057Ø403

To teach the child

>to *feel* beauty,

>to *love* beauty,

>to *seek* beauty,

>to *find* beauty,

are fundamentals of a sound

art program in the elementary grades.

Dedicated to Dr. Ira Jarrell, Superintendent, and to the Principals and Teachers of the Atlanta Elementary Schools, whose inspiration and friendship I shall always cherish.

Creative
Expression
with
Crayons

ELISE REID BOYLSTON

Formerly, Supervisor of Art, Atlanta Elementary Schools, Atlanta, Georgia

Davis Publications, Inc.
Printers Building, Worcester, Massachusetts

COPYRIGHT 1954

BY DAVIS PUBLICATIONS, INC.,

WORCESTER, MASS., U.S.A.

SIXTH PRINTING — 1964

Library of Congress Catalog Card Number 55-18220

Preface

Since emphasis has been placed upon the personality development of the child rather than upon the finished product, there have been varying opinions as to the best methods by which art should be taught; so it is little wonder that the classroom teacher is at times somewhat confused.

Art has long been considered by many administrators and taxpayers as a frill; and the requirements for teacher-training have not stressed, in many institutions, equal preparation in art education as for other subjects. The result has been to throw the inexperienced teacher into situations for which she is wholly or partly unprepared. She needs immediate and definite assistance. In many school systems there is no art consultant or coordinator of whom she can ask help; so no matter how eager she is to use the best methods of teaching art she is often perplexed and perhaps confused as to the correct procedure.

For average children of elementary school level, there is no art medium more economical or readily available, more delightful and satisfying to the child, or easier to manipulate than the colored crayon.

Since children's tastes and aptitudes differ, a wide variety of art materials should be provided wherever possible in order to allow free selection and exploration of media. But especially when finances are limited, crayons and large-sized paper become excellent basic material for elementary school art; and they are probably the most widely used medium in the elementary schools of today. The broad side of the crayon lends itself to big sweeps and free arm movement. The point gives accent, and with different degrees of pressure and unlimited variety of strokes, sparkling exciting effects can be produced.

The author, who has had broad experience as a teacher-trainer and a supervisor of art, has chosen this subject in order to lighten the load of the grade teacher by giving her a clearer understanding of the correct approach to child development through the use of crayons. The text explains how children think and work, and gives methods for stimulation and guidance. Ideas are suggested, not for copying any particular method but to furnish guides by which the teacher may know the kinds of art projects that children enjoy and thereby stimulate them to originate others. It is hoped this book will promote creative thinking, and motivate art through other mediums as well as through crayons.

By following the general activities outlined, the teacher will work out her own original methods of creative leadership. Through understanding the meaning of child art, together with the attendant enrichment of her own personality, she will not rely upon patterns or other outmoded methods of teaching; but will be equipped more completely to inspire and to lead those entrusted to her care.

Acknowledgment

Special acknowledgment is made to Mrs. Esther deLemos Morton, Editor, 1950–1953, and Miss Jane Rehnstrand, Associate Editor, 1942–1953, of the *School Arts* Magazine, for their wonderful advice and assistance in the selection and assembling of material; and to *School Arts* Magazine for the use of their illustrations.

Grateful acknowledgment is also made to the teachers and pupils of Spring Street School, Atlanta, for illustrations; and to the Principal, Mrs. Harold Douglas, and the Art Teacher, Mrs. Juliette Maxwell, for their gracious help and cooperation. Acknowledgment is also made to Mrs. Leone Bowers Hamilton, Art Teacher in DeKalb County, Georgia; and to others who have helped so willingly to make this book possible.

Contents

When finished, these imaginary birds in heavy, brilliant crayon technique were covered with wax paper to give the design a parchment effect.
Ruth Laughlin, Teacher, Third Grade, San Anselmo, California

Crayon Drawing Can Be Dramatic!

IN ORDER that the children may become fully acquainted with the medium, ample opportunity should be provided in the elementary grades for playing with crayons, investigating the different types used, and exploring their possibilities for dramatic adventure.

The crayon should be presented to the child in such a way as to capture his immediate interest, and encourage him to seek original methods of expression. It has exciting possibilities, and should be introduced to bring about an appreciation and an awareness of its many uses.

Technique is an expression of individuality, and should not be imposed. It is acquired by the child and used as a tool with which to express more easily and richly. The young child is inventive and resourceful and needs no suggestion for its use. For mechanical and involved methods such as setting colors in textiles, or when older children feel the need of improving their skill, and ask for help, simple demonstrations may be given, especially when new types of crayons, such as those having the effect of oil or water color, are being introduced.

Much experimentation on the part of the child is necessary in acquiring ease and understanding. He should try to discover how many different ways he can use the crayons to produce new shapes and combinations; accenting with the point, working with the blunt end, and turning the crayon around in a circle like a fan. By applying heavier pressure on one side, graduated and shaded strokes result. Trailing, rhythmic, and dancing lines add interest. Layers of varying colors, or the same color, may be piled one on the other to give the effect of oils; and closely-related colors may be blended for subtle and pleasing arrangements.

Smooth and rough papers bring about different results; and colored or bogus papers are a never-ending source of interesting backgrounds. Notches cut in the side of the crayon give a broken line, and when rubbed against an uneven surface such as wire-screen or sandpaper, a textured effect is produced. Experiments should be made with long and short pieces of crayon, and with dark and light colors, bright and dull combinations, blended hues, and colors applied over each other and scratched for an etched effect. Experimentation is full of exciting possibilities, especially in the upper grades where the children are "a-tiptoe" for new and individual methods of expression.

Masses of color blended over the paper produce new shapes, movements and relationships. These abstract compositions may be used to cover portfolios or other craft objects, since children derive satisfaction in putting their drawings to further use. In this way, mere experimentation with crayons may lead to a well-rounded unit in construction.

Pencil lines around a crayon drawing are artificial. They are tight and prevent spontaneous expression. Drawing and coloring should be done directly on the paper with the crayons. Through trial and error, the child may discover that outlining an area with black or white or colored crayons gives a decorative touch and helps to emphasize. A wax crayon

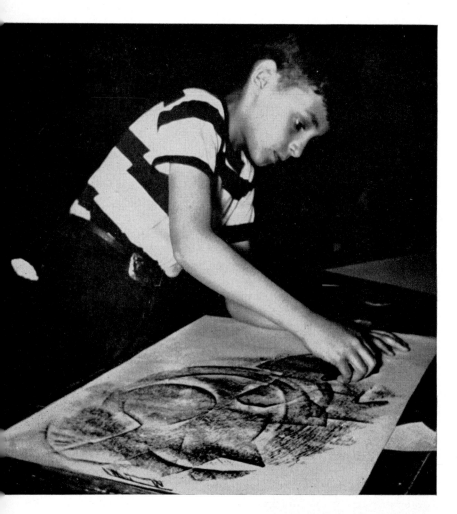

RUBBED DESIGNS—
Billy is fascinated with
what is appearing on
his paper. Broken
crayons were peeled
and the broad side
used. The children had
cut all sorts of abstract
shapes from manila
paper which, when cov-
ered with newsprint
and rubbed with a
black crayon, produced
dramatic designs.

Jessie Todd, Teacher
University of
Chicago Laboratory
School

WHITE ON BLACK—White crayon or chalk
on black paper gives very dramatic results.
Myrtle G. Sanders
Art Instructor and Supervisor
High School Level
Sault Ste. Marie, Michigan

DOG AND CAT—By using a crayon on its side and applying heavier pressure on one end than on the other, broad-stroke is achieved.

Alice Marland
Elementary Art Supervisor
Ossining, New York

line around certain areas serves also to hold in water-color washes when that medium is added, preventing the paint from spreading.

The outline, however, must not be overdone. It becomes a "crutch" when depended upon too often for emphasis and contrast. It may also appear artificial and monotonous. If the child has a tendency to over-outline his figures, the teacher should encourage a diversity of color and different widths of line, instead of the one black outline. Variety of all kinds is necessary in making the composition a success.

There should be no set rules for using the crayon. No directions for drawing or using definite colors or methods of work should be given; but the teacher should be alert in acting as counselor and guide. Left to create without interference, the child will discover for himself original ways of using the crayon. He will feel that he is having a thrilling adventure in expressing his individual ideas and reactions to the world around him. This self-directed exploration will be recalled and used by him later in creating new skills and original methods of working with colored crayons.

You Don't Have To Be An Artist!

EVERY grade teacher should be able to stimulate children to creative expression through art. Any teacher who desires to teach this subject successfully can do so. She need not be an artist. She does not have to know how to draw or paint. The ability to express readily through art media is undoubtedly of help; but success in the classroom depends upon the teacher herself—on her interest and resourcefulness in planning interesting approaches; on correct evaluation of her own methods, and the progress made by the class. A sincere desire to meet and satisfy the child's needs, rather than his achievement of skill or the finished product, is more vital to the success of the grade teacher than any artistic talent which she might possess.

It is significant that all children enjoy art today as never before; and parents speak enthusiastically of their child's ability to draw. This is evidence that the real objectives in art education are being reached, and that the methods in present-day use are successfully accomplishing their purpose.

One of the most important qualifications of a successful grade teacher of art is the ability to recognize the difference between imitation and creative expression. She must understand and appreciate child art and its relation to the development of personality. She must know the objectives toward which to work and be able to formulate methods that will stimulate and guide the child for happy learning. A desire to improve her teaching skills by reading the latest books recommended for art education will help to keep her informed on contemporary developments, accepted methods, and changing trends.

Art is the richest and most delightful of subjects. When once the teacher has sensed the freshness and originality of the creative expression of the child, she will have no further use for sterile or formal methods of teaching. She will realize that dependence upon traced work, filling in hectographed outlines, or copying pictures, either directly or recalled, will inhibit the child and limit his initiative and ability to think for himself. She will know that forcing adult ideas upon him will lessen his own creative powers. She will learn that adverse criticism will rob him of self-confidence, and projects that require the whole class to do the same thing in the same way are deadening to originality and imagination.

Creative expression demands an entirely different type of approach. It encourages the child to experiment and investigate. It strives to give him confidence to initiate and invent. It attempts to develop his powers of expression, and helps him to live happily and cooperatively with others. It involves critical thinking and careful planning, as well as thoughtful evaluation of his own work.

Since art activity plays such a vital part in personality growth, the teacher should study the individual needs of the child. By understanding his free creative expressions, she will know what type of help to give. She will realize that drawings of conflict and wish-fulfillment evidence need for careful guidance. She will use creative art expression as a medium for helping the maladjusted child. By recognizing and interpreting characteristics of each child's manner of working, she will guide him constructively and encourage him to further develop his individual aptitudes, skills and personality.

To this end, the teacher should lead the child to originate and solve his problems and to think for himself. Her function is to help him recreate his own experiences and record them in graphic form instead of imposing her own plans and adult ideas upon him. Spontaneous expression of an experience frees the child, and his inner feelings are released. When there is satisfaction in drawing, there will be growth. When there is joy in the result, there will be further urge for activity. By praising honest effort, expressing confidence in the child's ability to create, and finding her own joy and recompense in the work, she will lead the child to steady self-development of the potentialities that lie within him. She guides, inspires, encourages and appreciates; and she finds that initiative

You Don't Have To Be An Artist!

and skill will evolve naturally through actual experience, and from trial and error. She visions what art education can do for the child in developing his mental and spiritual self, in aiding him to adjust happily to his environment, and to work toward higher ideals and standards of living.

A danger in stressing creative expression is for the inexperienced teacher to accept whatever the child does, and feel that it is good because he works without direction. Creative leadership does not suggest that the child be left entirely alone to draw as he pleases without supervision. This would be license, and not the type of freedom that is intended. The child must have skillful guidance and encouragement all along the way—skillful because too much supervision results in formal drawing, and too much freedom without stimulation ends in stagnation.

Dr. Harold Rice has aptly said, "The teaching of art is an art"; and it is the conscientious teacher, the dynamic teacher, the teacher who loves her work, who succeeds in developing the mental, the social, and the emotional personality of the whole child.

Decorating the letters of the alphabet can serve as motivation for wax crayon experiments as well as penmanship interrelation.

Sister Mary Azeveda, Teacher, Toledo, Ohio

HOLDING THE CRAYON—There are two natural positions of holding wax or chalk crayons.

1. With the crayon held upright, one may achieve fine lines with its tapered end, or a broader, even stroke with the blunt end.

2. Broad, shaded strokes may be produced by using the crayon on its side, with more pressure exerted on one end than the other.

Jane Rehnstrand, State Teachers College, Superior, Wisconsin

14

Exciting Methods Of Using Crayons!

SIMPLY drawing with crayons on large sheets of paper is the most widely used method of handling this medium; but there are many other delightful ways of working with the various types of crayons. Among these are stenciling, crayon etching, crayon batik, textile coloring, wood staining and decorating, transferring designs, coloring stereopticon slides, and producing oil, pastel, and water-color effects. The child beginning a new method for the first time finds it an exciting experience. In order that the teacher may understand these methods and lead the child correctly, directions are given to increase facility in carrying out different types of work. The crayon is a versatile medium that lends itself to many types of strokes. The broad side of the unwrapped crayon is similar to chalk in covering background or solid areas. Light, medium, and dark surfaces are achieved through varying degrees of pressure, and variety is shown by grading the surface from dark to light. A third dimension may be shown also in this way. The point may be used like a pencil for sketching or accenting edges and for showing different types of textures.

Wax Resist Washes

The wax resist is made by drawing the design heavily in bright colors, leaving the paper blank where the solid areas are to be. Black or colored waterproof ink or transparent or opaque water colors are floated over the surface to fill in the unwaxed parts, leaving a soft lovely texture and a delightful blending of colors. Another interesting method of using the wax resist is outlining the design with white or pink crayons and dipping the paper into bluing. Other contrasts of color may be chosen by individuals.

Crayon "Etching"

Etching is a technical term applied to engraving by eating out the design with acid in preparing a copper plate for making an etching print. A process akin to the wax resist design and somewhat resembling a zinc etching is the crayon "etching" which is made by covering a smooth-finished paper with a heavy film of wax crayon, and adding successive layers of contrasting colors over the first. Scratching through the different layers with a sharp point or orangewood stick gives an interesting texture. Original designs using this technique, and attractively mounted, would be a welcome gift for each mother who attends the Parent-Teacher meeting.

Transfer Designs

A design may be transferred easily by outlining it heavily with wax crayon on the back to reverse the design. Laid face-down on the paper or cloth and pressed with a hot iron, the original may be repeated. This method is not recommended for regular use since the free drawing of repeats is more casual and pleasing. However, it may be useful in certain instances.

FOUR METHODS OF USING CRAYONS—*Upper left:* Wax crayon line tinted with water color. *Upper right:* Line textures in two colors of wax crayon. *Lower left:* A broadstroke illustration. *Lower right:* Crayon or chalk dust used through a stencil.

Frances L. Stokes, Art Supervisor, Ely, Minnesota

Rubbed Designs

Rubbed designs are made by placing a thin sheet of colored or white paper over one or more rough objects to be copied or transferred, such as cord or paper shapes, and the crayon rubbed back and forth over the surface. The raised parts are thus reproduced on paper. By blending several colors, lovely effects in shading may be created with autumn leaves as allover designs. With tempera floated over such a design, made perhaps with cord, interesting cover papers result. Allover patterns in stripes can be made by cutting one or both edges of a thin strip of cardboard so that the edge forms a design, then laying it under a colored paper and rubbing the crayon away from the edges to etch the design. The strip is moved about to form the repeat.

Gift Wrappings

Gift-wrapping paper may be made by drawing repeats with crayons on tissue or other suitable wrapping paper. An attractive combination of color and design is made by spattering the paper with gold or silver paint, either before or after it is decorated with crayons.

Stenciling

The design to be stenciled is cut from tough paper such as commercial stencils or the backs of mimeograph stencils. The cutout portions are held against the background paper or cloth and the crayon rubbed carefully through the holes and close to the edges to make a definite outline. In combining a number of colors, only one stencil is needed. A graded effect is produced by shading and blending the colors carefully through the openings.

Stencils may also be shaded from an outline, away from a curved or straight edge. The stencil may be moved about

to make allover or border repeats which are especially effective in non-objective design.

Stenciled Murals

Stencils may be used successfully with young children in making large murals. They first draw a house or other object and cut it out to make a silhouette, which is then traced and cut from lightweight cardboard. The resulting hole forms the stencil through which the painting is done. Small pieces of crayon are melted to a liquid which is painted through the stencil. The resulting wash is solid and shiny, and produces an unusual effect. These stencils are large and may be moved over the paper for a mural and repeated any number of times to cover large surfaces quickly. Gray oatmeal paper makes a pleasing background. In arranging the units, a sense of composition is developed. The brushes must be thoroughly cleansed in turpentine after using.

Crayon Painting

A method of painting directly on paper or cloth is done with large brushes and melted crayons. If desired, water colors may be used with the crayon units, and is suitable for young children as well as those more advanced. This method gives an interesting effect.

Crayon Shavings

In sharpening crayons for making fine lines, shavings collect, and these can be put to use in decorative design by sprinkling them over plain or colored paper, covering the whole with newsprint, and running a warm iron over it to melt the crayon.

Wax Resist Wash   *Paper Batik*

Mrs. Juliette Maxwell, Art Teacher, Spring Street School, Atlanta, Georgia

ETCHED CRAYON—Areas were coated with a thick layer of wax crayon, then all was coated with black india ink. A uniform texture of scratchboard technique allows a good showing of color and unifies the design.

Marion Modena, Teacher
Saturday Art Class, twelve-year-olds, California College of Arts and Crafts

Crayons Melted With Paraffin

Modeling may be done with softened wax crayons mixed with paraffin. This mixture, melted, may also be used in decorating lamp shades, booklet covers, favors, and greeting folders.

Paper Batik

Paper batik is made by drawing the design heavily with wax crayons. The paper is dipped into water to soften so it will not crack, and it is crumpled in the hands. Then it is straightened and a contrasting color floated over it, either with water-color solution, or thinly dissolved crayons. A warm iron is run over it while still wet or nearly dry. If a more crinkled effect is desired, the four corners should be pinned down and the paper allowed to dry naturally. By using brown wrapping paper and brown crayons, the effect of leather is produced. This is nice for covering portfolios.

Textiles

Textiles may be colored with wax crayons, either drawn freely or with the use of a stencil. The strokes should follow the fibers of the cloth. Alternating light and dark areas give contrast and striking effects; covering with a damp cloth and running a warm iron over the design will set the color. This is a delightful method of design when outlined with colored floss or thread in different stitches. The colors will not fade if washed in warm soap flakes.

Textile Batik

Textile batik is quite popular for luncheon mats or allover design. The crayon is applied heavily and, if the fabric is thin, color is applied to the back also. The cloth is then dipped into cold-

RUBBED DESIGN—Several figures cut from manila paper were arranged in allover pattern. Newsprint was then laid over the figures and rubbed with the broad side of a peeled wax crayon

Jessie Todd, Teacher
Sixth Grade, University of Chicago
Laboratory School

Exciting Methods Of Using Crayons!

SANDPAPER PAINTING—Wax crayon on No. 1 or No. 2 sandpaper.

Geraldine E. Meyers, Teacher
Junior High School, Kirksville, Missouri

Creative Expression with Crayons

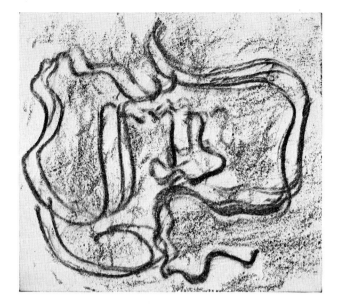

CRAYON AND STRING—String design motifs may be arrested by covering them with lightweight paper and rubbing over it with the side of a crayon.

Jessie Todd, Teacher
Fifth Grade
University of Chicago
Laboratory School

water dye and crushed in the hands. If a softer color is desired, the cloth is dipped in gasoline.

Folded Paper Designs

Half of a design may be drawn heavily on one side of a folded paper and pressed with a hot iron to duplicate it on the other half.

Tooling

Tooling is done by laying a sheet of paper over a damp padding and pressing a line decoration into the paper with a nutpick, making a bas-relief design, which is then filled in with crayons.

Paper Plates

Paper plates are convenient for holding nuts or popcorn, and may be used at Halloween or other special occasions. The circular form lends itself well to design, and may be decorated with wax crayon in combination with melted crayons or paint.

Sandpaper and Crayons

Working directly on sandpaper gives an interesting effect. Fine sandpaper is excellent for sharpening crayons also.

Crackled Paper

Crackled paper is made by crumpling a piece of paper under water. It is smoothed out and painted a light color with dissolved crayons. Then it is reversed and painted a darker color on the other side. The color will seep through and give a mottled effect.

Oil Crayons

Oil crayons give the effect of oil paint as well as being used as ordinary crayons. They may be blended with the fingers or with a brush dipped in turpentine, gasoline, or mineral spirits. A non-inflammable fluid is best in the classroom.

Oil crayons are interesting for outdoor sketching. They may be dipped directly into the solvent, and the colors applied over each other or piled in relief,

20

simulating oil paint, or the solvent applied to the finished drawing. The colors are vibrant, and work equally well on paper or cloth. By melting the shavings and mixing with kerosene or turpentine, the color may be floated on top of a pan of water and the paper pulled through the water to give a marbled effect.

Water Soluble Crayons

Water-soluble crayons cost little, are brilliant, and have a variety of uses. They may be applied like regular crayons. By floating a wash of plain water over a drawing, or by working on damp paper, a water-color effect is produced.

Exciting Methods Of Using Crayons!

Where a crisp finish is desired, a combination of crayons and water colors may be made by adding water to certain areas only.

Water soluble crayons may be used on fabrics by stretching the cloth over a damp blotter or by wetting the fabric itself and applying the crayons. This makes a smooth finish. Dissolved in water, they may be used with a brush to give the effect of regular water colors. They make a rich stain for wood or leather. They may be painted or rubbed

CRAYON PAINTING—With sufficient precaution, melted wax crayons afford a stimulating medium for upper level students. The effect is that of thick oil paint. Softening the end of a crayon by candle flame is a practical method of painting with wax crayons in the classroom.

Nelle R. McGee, Art Instructor, City Schools, Evansville, Indiana

Creative Expression with Crayons

into the material, following the grain, and buffed with a damp cloth. Pressing hard against the wood surface with a cloth produces a lighter effect.

Pastel Crayons

Pastel crayons are soft and do not rub off as easily as chalk, but they give somewhat the same effect if used on the side for softly blended effects.

Staining Wood With Oil Crayons

Wood may be stained by being cov-ered with a smooth wax film and wiped with a piece of cloth dipped in gasoline. This gives an even stain, after which the box or other article may be decorated with a crayon design. It should be finished with a coat of wax.

These are some of the stimulating methods of using various kinds of crayons. Other techniques may be learned or worked out through experimentation. However, this explanation furnishes a basis for the teacher who may not be familiar with the many available types of crayons and their use.

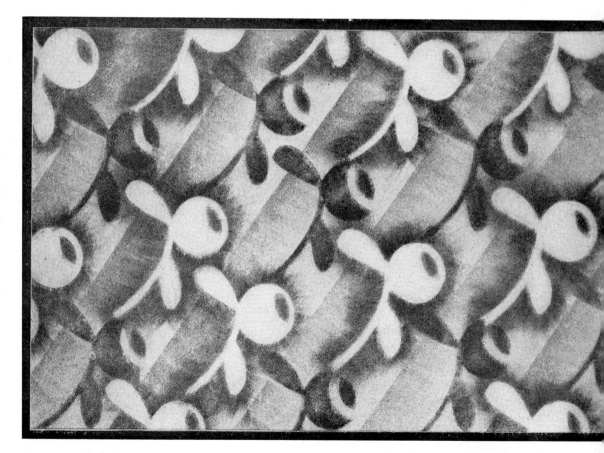

A chalk-type crayon design.

Morton High School, Cicero, Illinois

Children like to experiment with using crayons in many ways.   The problem here was to completely fill a square and to press on the crayon for strong color accent.

Top left: Grade 3-a, Hamilton School, Minneapolis, Minnesota
All others by Grade 2, Elementary School, University of Chicago, Jessie Todd, Art Instructor

Large chalk-type crayons and big pieces of paper make colorful Mother Goose murals.

Winifred Robinson, Teacher—Mary D. Reed, Art Supervisor

First Grade, Hamilton Schools, Minneapolis, Minnesota

Color

Can Be

Stimulating!

APPRECIATION and understanding of color are developed through observation and use as well as the personal reaction of the individual. Since the young child has no previous associations of color, he chooses it for its immediate appeal, and the green or red that he prefers for his elephant is more plausible to him than the realistic brown or gray of the creature he has never seen.

As environmental influences begin to be felt, he selects dull or gay colors according to his moods. A happy child selects warm, sunny hues, while a child from drab surroundings might choose more neutral tones.

Color creates mood, it symbolizes ideas, it attracts attention. It is an emotional stimulus—a type of symbolism. Children should be left free to select and use colors without suggestions or adult interference. For the child awakened to the message that color has for him, there will be joyous response and an added delight in creative drawing.

Experimentation with crayons plays a large part in developing a sensitivity to different combinations of hue, and the personality of the child unfolds in turn through its use. In the symbolic stage, he is interested in color for its own sake, and plays with it for pure enjoyment; therefore, ample opportunity should be provided for playing with and exploring the possibilities of color. To develop an awareness and appreciation, he should be encouraged to select and enjoy pleasing combinations in the productions of classmates and the works of noted artists.

Color experiences should be emotional. The freedom of the early years should be encouraged so the child will continue to feel color intuitively and use it by choice rather than representation.

There exist no rigid color theories that will not hamper free expression. The use of charts and formulas results in stilted unexciting combinations, and limits the child's imagination and response to his own interpretation of hue.

Every individual reacts differently to color stimulus. The visually-minded child prefers naturalistic rendering, whereas the non-visual type uses color as he feels it. Therefore, choice of hue differs with the type of individual exposed to it. In order to preserve the freedom of expression desired and to guide the child intelligently in its use, the teacher should be aware of certain facts and significant ideas about it.

In using crayons, no suggestions whatever are needed. Left alone, children naturally select the hues which serve best to interpret their feelings and ideas. The teacher who understands the effect of environment, and is able to recognize inhibitions and expressions of poorly-adjusted children through their use of color and line can do much to direct them to normality, and further their development through art expression.

In the class discussion which follows a period of experimentation, children learn the effect of colors upon each other, which hues combine pleasingly, and what reactions are brought about, such as striking and dynamic effect of contrast— warm colors against cool, and darks

25

Creative Expression with Crayons

against lights. This produces a feeling of movement and action. They may see how color helps to interpret certain qualities such as daintiness and softness of face-powder, or fear and foreboding in expressions of danger. Because of its emotional effect upon the individual, color plays a vital and significant role in all life situations. In advertising, a poster for butter may use greens and yellows to signify the sun, the rich Jersey cream, and the luscious green fields in which the cows graze.

As children use color consciously to carry out certain ideas and impressions, and are interested in its significance, they require guidance to build a sensitivity to its use and an understanding of its possibilities. Color expression should not be discussed as a thing apart. It should be integrated with life situations, and used as a response to a recognized need. By studying good pictures to interpret the artist's message as well as by analyzing one's personal reactions to color, the child will learn that different hues and values have varying effects; that they create different moods and emotions, and that color speaks a language of its own.

Colors may be decorative or realistic. It is not necessary that grass be green or skies be blue. The vitality and beauty of the whole range of color are open to the child's imagination, and should be his for the choosing.

Interpretive color is imaginative and helps to provide the keynote of a picture. A giraffe may be painted green if the child deems that hue best suited to express what he is trying to say. Perhaps the adult may not agree with the child's taste, but neither can he know how the child feels or thinks. If decorative color-

ing calls for purple dots and green clover leaves on a garden variety of pig, that is as it should be if the child wishes it so.

Colors are designated as warm or cool. Yellow, red, and orange are commonly known as warm colors. However, colors are relative and are affected, in the final analysis, by other hues used with them. Blue is considered a cool color. Green and purple are either warm or cool since they are a combination of both warm and cool colors.

Cool colors are calm and retiring, and if grayed, they tend to become weird and mysterious. Warm colors are stimulating and aggressive, noisy and exciting. Balance is found in compositions that are made up of both warm and cool tones with either predominating to set the mood. The child feels these things instinctively. He does not know why. He would be unable to express the reason. He chooses the colors he feels should be used, and the teacher who is able to understand this basic trait and also her own personal reactions to color will be better able to guide children intelligently. They, however, have no reason for learning mere terms. They should feel the stimulus of color. They should make their own choice, and use it to their personal development and unfolding of their total personality.

Through the ages, color has taken on psychological meaning through the association of ideas. For the child awakened to the message that color holds for him, it proves a delightful and joy-giving companion. The use of color in stained-glass windows would be a most profitable and interesting study in the upper elementary grades. Here, the meaning attached to biblical characters is indicated through choice of hue which reflects the personality and other attributes in a subtle and emotional way.

The main idea or center of interest in a composition may be emphasized by use of strong color and unique combinations. Repeated colors as well as forms in different areas of a picture help to produce balance; and the artist's meaning is interpreted through color schemes, tones, tints and shades. Backgrounds should bring out the main objects through the use of contrast; grayed colors on the edges of a composition emphasize this primary interest further.

For sense realization, children should be made conscious of color in Christmas lights. They should feel the movements and hues in crowds; see rhythm and color in smoke; enjoy the changing values of blue and violet, green, red and yellow in soap bubbles; notice brilliant colors in skies and sunsets, wondrous hues that flash forth in rocks under fluorescent light, and pattern and color that result from erosion. They should see the glory of autumn trees and the rich weathered brown of a gnarled fence post. They should seek color everywhere.

Children should be encouraged to use their crayons to invent new color schemes and try for unusual combinations and exotic arrangements in shade and hue. Instead of the traditional outline of black, they may experiment with striking colors—turquoise and magenta and red. They should suggest interesting color

Color Can Be Stimulating!

schemes for using crayons—a white or yellow cat on a blue-green rug; chartreuse water and violet coral and green seaweed against blue rocks, with black fish swimming about. They should thrill to such color arrangements as a slinky, black panther silhouetted against an orange rock, or white-clothed Eskimos with blue sky and penguins with orange feet and black wings. Mental pictures such as these produce strong visual impressions and vigorous striking contrasts. But the child should not be limited to brilliant colors. Blonds usually prefer pastel colors while brunettes are partial to the warm tones with values similar to their coloring. This is largely due to the selection of colors that are becoming to the individual.

Color choice should be left to the child. It should reflect his emotional life and hold the key to his inhibitions and hopes. Brilliant or delicate, the drawing should be forceful and full of meaning. Too long have crayon drawings been anemic, inadequate pieces of work. Color and materials should fulfill their functions at all times. Being conscious of color everywhere and making whatever one sees a part of himself, an appreciation will develop to the child's happiness in living, and reflect the joy of working with crayons in his original art work.

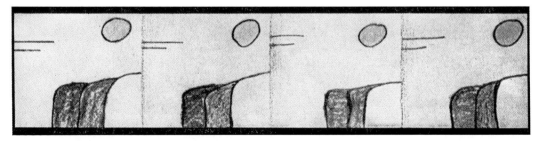

A wax crayon border design by second grade student.
Lois Tramm, Teacher, Snohomish, Washington

How
The Child
Works

IN THE natural development of the child, he passes through certain stages of growth, and has a definite pattern of working. These are necessary to his development; and adverse criticism only confuses or interrupts the free flow of ideas. If the child is not ready for the next step, he must not be pushed.

The sun is a seeming *must* to the child in practically every drawing, and is often placed in the corner. At times, balance is attained through two suns—one in each upper corner.

In most early pictures, the sky and grass do not meet. The child sees the sky above, the grass below, and the air between. The meeting of sky and ground will take care of itself when the child's observation has developed an awareness of it.

Children draw what they believe to be true, and not what they see; therefore, they draw smoke rising inside the chimney and two ends of the house at the same time because both are significant to them. Chimneys as the child knows them are made to carry off smoke. Telling him to draw them upright only confuses him because his mentality will not

Children draw in large size the things which seem most important to them. Note the tiny people looking on.
Mrs. Juliette Maxwell, Art Teacher, Spring Street School, Atlanta, Georgia

"Bus Stop"—Children are fond of repetition, as is shown in these figures. It is an outlet for their natural love of rhythm.

Mrs. Juliette Maxwell, Art Teacher, Spring Street School, Atlanta, Georgia

understand the double significance, and he cannot understand the reason for their position on the house.

The child emphasizes the thing that has last engaged his interest, and seems most important to him at the moment. A running child may have legs but no arms because it does not need them in running, and the necessity is not felt when he draws the picture. The reaching paw of a dog may be twice as long as the other legs to show its function and to emphasize reach.

Children have a natural feeling for balance and design, and they often distort an object consciously in order to achieve this satisfactorily to themselves. Color is chosen for its appeal and because the child thinks it best serves his purpose. Red elephants, therefore, are perfectly acceptable.

The very young child sees objects separately and scatters them over the paper without relationship to each other. He is not aware of the separate things as a unit, and does not put them together until he has realized this. At this stage in drawing, he is not ready to read since he cannot assemble words in their relationship to the whole.

A great deal can be understood about the child through his drawings; and the type of stimulus he needs at different stages of development can be determined. Because the child must not be discouraged or confused at this early age, the teacher should be familiar with these and other natural ways of working in order to give him the kind of stimulation and guidance he requires for building a happy foundation in creative art.

Art Expression In The Lower Elementary Grades

ART expression is a vitally important factor in the personality development of the child; and one of its most significant functions is to provide emotional release. It adds enjoyment to the life of the individual, helps him to recognize and appreciate what is good in art, and to be conscious of beauty wherever he finds it.

In the early part of the child's school experience, the symbolic stage is centered in self and things that touch his life most closely—the family, the home, his toys, his pets. The world is new and wonderful to him; and every happening is so significant and vital that he wants to relive it on paper and share it with others.

In the lower elementary grades, books, stories, poems, games, family happenings and activities—all furnish vivid mental pictures that help the child to become better acquainted with his environment. Colors and objects in nature especially appeal to him; and he is conscious of swirling smoke, sounds of wind and rain, and the color and odor of flowers. Trains and machinery, farm life, soldiers and animals intrigue him; and ordinary happenings tend to develop his powers of observation, and broaden his visual and mental vocabulary. Expression through art brings his imaginary and factual world to reality. The teacher will find in the child's own experiences rich material with which to guide him socially, mentally, and spiritually for democratic and satisfactory living.

The child's mind is like a sponge. When his interest is aroused, he spills over into oral and graphic expression. If he feels free to use his imagination as he pleases to record personal reactions, drawing becomes a delightful adventure. Sympathetic confidence in his ability to express gives him courage and a feeling that his efforts will be understood and appreciated, and activates in him an answering response in fresh, spontaneous work.

Enthusiasm on the part of the teacher helps to create an eagerness for art expression by the pupil. She encourages the child to plan and evaluate with her. Teaching is incidental until the critical stage is evident. A program that provides for every child to participate happily, and feel that he is succeeding, will necessarily bring about a natural development of the total personality and integration of self.

The first step in creative expression is getting acquainted with art materials at hand. Since children express more readily in certain mediums than others, they should be allowed a choice of those with which to work, but crayons are found to be entirely satisfactory for all children to nine years of age, and many prefer them at all ages.

In the motor and manipulative stages, the child learns what he can do with crayons and paper. Simple movements of the crayon over the paper intrigue him until he passes into the symbolic and the realistic stages. Abstract play of color is the result. As he approaches the representative stage, he draws things, not as he sees them, but as he believes them to

"LAND OF ENCHANTMENT"—"Art is the very young student's land of enchantment. Creating it, he discovers a wonderland of beautiful forms, patterns, and colors. Exploring it, he finds himself, and by this self-discovery fulfills the aim of art education."

Ada Bel Beckwith, Supervisor of Art, Lakewood, Ohio

be. His experiences are so vital that they furnish adequate material for creative expression; therefore, the illustration of stories told or read should be used only occasionally as need arises in the lower elementary grades.

Boys draw guns and gangsters and planes and cowboys, while girls show home activities, holiday seasons, and everyday happenings. Interest in self broadens to other peoples, fantastic ideas, nonsense, and even to mild humor in the more advanced children of the lower grades.

While stimulation must be constant, there is never reason to show the child how or what to draw. Thinking for him only makes him rely less upon his own initiative; and showing him how tends to impose the teacher's own ideas and techniques upon him. The natural result is for him to imitate adult methods

or try to please. The teacher should set the stage by providing a sympathetic environment that will invite true creativity. She should use the child's own interests as motivation, and urge him to express his personal interpretation of the things that most vitally touch his life. She should help him to observe closely; and through conversation and other methods, arouse his curiosity to seek new ideas and trends of thought. She should not worry about skills or correct draftsmanship. These are acquired through experience and constructive guidance along the way. Emphasis should be placed upon her own attitude toward the child's work—what she expects from him and what she can give in return. Her role is to provide interesting material that challenges the imagination; and she must stimulate him to recall significant events and develop original ideas and

"THE FARMYARD" by a seven-year-old—Barnyard birds appeal to the young child who finds their varied shapes and colors an appealing outlet for his creativeness.

Lorraine Goff Le Sueur, Director of Children's Classes
Walker Art Center, Minneapolis, Minn.

Creative Expression with Crayons

ways of expressing them. She must help him to control his materials with greater ease.

It is important that the teacher judge the child's results from his point of view rather than that of the adult. She respects his efforts as worthy, and accepts his own interpretation of life.

The experiences and emotions of children are so vivid that they leave strong impressions; and these ideas make up a vast store of interesting material upon which the teacher may draw for art expression. If encouraged and left to explore and create freely, the child will express his reactions to his environment in his own unique way. His drawings will be forthright and sincere.

Progress is the result of selecting subject matter wisely and solving the problems that naturally arise. But art awareness does not progress without guidance. If left to draw without stimulation, interest and imagination lag. Even the younger child is quick to realize when he is making no progress; and his enthusiasm for manipulation and the enjoyment of color diminishes as subject matter grows stale and he becomes less creative. He is unable to visualize his mental pictures clearly enough to recreate them, and continues to draw the same people and trees and houses with no variety of expression or feeling of satisfaction to himself. This phase of inactivity, however, must not be confused with that in which the child uses repetition to give him a feeling of security by convincing himself that he can reproduce his former drawings at will. This conscious power over materials affords him definite satisfaction; but in stagnation, there is lack of interest; and when this is evident, it is time for outside stimulation and guidance to be used.

Imagination in the lower elementary grades is strong, and the young child draws the impossible as readily as he pictures the realistic. A normal child naturally draws happy pictures, but environment continues to exert a strong influence over choice of subject matter.

Certain suggestions from time to time help him to express more easily, use color more freely, draw large objects and fill the paper more satisfactorily. However, too much attention to methods of working tends to hamper free expression; so these ideas must be brought out in class discussion during the evaluation period after the lesson. Merely calling attention to and commending what is good emphasizes them sufficiently. But as children progress, they should be encouraged to mention at the beginning of the lesson some of the principles they have found to be worthwhile which have improved their drawings.

Art Expression In The Lower Elementary Grades

Calling attention incidentally to such art principles as darks against lights for contrast, good composition, strong execution, and interesting subject matter and color as they occur in the drawings, helps to make these ideas a part of the child's working knowledge so he will tend to use them unconsciously as he draws.

The time to help the child is when he realizes the need and seeks assistance. Skillful questioning aids him to solve his problems. Short simple demonstrations may be given when the need is felt. Thus, through encouragement, experimentation, and discussion, the child is stimulated to express his own ideas in his own way. Therefore, to bring about satisfaction in accomplishment and a broader vision and acquaintance with the world about him, the child should be guided and encouraged to see more things, use interesting subject matter in his own way, and derive pleasure and a sense of accomplishment in creative expression with colored crayons.

This lower grade child's drawing of a caterpillar is just full of imagination and expression.

Opal K. Sloan, Elementary Art Coordinator
Lubbock, Texas

Art Expression In The Upper Elementary Grades

ART education in the upper elementary grades differs from that of the lower, largely in enrichment and broadening of subject matter and ideas. Naturally, there are improved skills, clearer understanding of methods and materials and more critical observation, with higher standards and greater interest in objects of utilitarian value. The children are concerned with things that touch their lives—the community with its shops and workers, objects of art with their design and color, new methods of using materials. But the objectives of all the elementary grades are the same—the development of personality and aesthetic sensitivity to color, mass, and line that will make for fuller and more satisfying living.

When the child has reached the fourth grade level, observation and initiative have been partially developed; and if allowed to create freely as he has been doing in the lower grades, the boy or girl expresses through graphic art almost as readily as he speaks. Then art has become truly a language, as well as a source of joy and an outlet for emotional stress.

While the young child is satisfied with crude results, and needs only guidance and stimulation, with ample opportunity to experiment, children of the third and fourth grade levels are emerging from the state of unawareness where drawing is direct and free to a more critical attitude because of awakened observation and outside influences. Their own emphasis shifts to the finished product rather than the process, and they grow more exacting in details as they seek to attain adult standards and skills to which they have been exposed through books and newspapers.

As observation grows keener, imagination becomes less active, and the importance of subject matter and improved skills begins to assert itself. The child has worked so freely with satisfactory results to himself in the lower elementary grades that he cannot understand why he is unable to express form realistically as he now desires, and he feels frustrated and dissatisfied. He realizes that his own drawings are less finished looking than the adult illustrations to which he has been exposed, that third dimension and perspective make objects appear to be different, and that he is unable to reach the standard which he sets for himself. He desires more definite knowledge of skills; therefore, he often requests help in solving his problems. This is the critical age; and unless he receives sympathetic encouragement and understanding, he loses interest and turns to copying.

Careful guidance at this stage is necessary to help the child make the transition from unconscious freedom to conscious activity and achievement so he will continue to believe in his own ability to produce worthy art. The teacher should encourage in him a feeling of making natural progress through creative expression. She should help him to visualize more clearly, to select subject matter more wisely, and to put emphasis

34

"Visit to the Beauty Parlor"—a natural subject for the girls.

In the upper grades the students are more interested in the subject matter than in the process, and they seek to attain adult standards of illustration.

Mrs. Juliette Maxwell, Art Teacher, Spring Street School, Atlanta, Georgia

on his intellectual and emotional development.

To prevent his drawings from becoming photographic, the teacher should encourage free creative activity; to give the boy or girl a sense of personal achievement and self-confidence in his own ability to express, so he will continue to want to draw. He must be made to feel that if his drawings do not meet his expectations, they will be stepping stones to better results. It is important to provide lively interest so imaginative qualities will be encouraged and original and dramatic expression will result.

Children of this age derive particular benefit from looking at pictures by various artists—Dufy, Michael Angelo, Van Gogh, Pieter Brueghel, and by enjoying Chinese prints. Attention should not be called to any particular

period, but to the many different ways in which landscapes, animals, or people can be portrayed. Children who are disturbed by not being able to draw figures as they wish, might find comfort in the street scenes by Utrillo where the figures suggest bulk and are definitely people although they may have no arms or legs—no features or detail.

At this critical stage, skills are necessary for progress; but attitudes and aesthetic awareness and growth can only be acquired through individual effort, and by seeing, doing, and evaluating through cooperation with the teacher. These objectives develop through the child's urge for expression. Children should be proud of their work, and to this end they are eager to have help in improving their skills. When the definite need is felt by the child, occasional

Creative Expression with Crayons

simple lessons in art instruction may be given by the teacher to insure greater confidence and joy in expression. Children get a tremendous thrill from discovering new ideas and ways of working; and they feel an immense sense of satisfaction in realizing good results. Whenever necessary, and only then, should art instruction be given in what is essential; and only then should art instruction be given in what is required to help develop the skill which the children are anxious to attain. Pictures of unfamiliar things may be shown also and discussed for understanding characteristics—the motion of animals; their slinkiness or bulk; their own particular features; the emotional effect of work done by different artists; good color combinations and how they affect the picture.

This stimulation should not be formal instruction but guidance which allows opportunity for originality and thoughtful planning. At times, there should be definite objectives in mind—to make large drawings that fill the page; to show overlapping to give a feeling of depth, as in crowds; to understand more clearly the approach to design and emotional expression; to draw people and animals more easily. The teacher should clarify the work, thus enabling the child to express more readily whatever he has in mind. If demonstrations are given by the teacher when necessity arises, not one but several methods should be shown so the child will not use any particular technique. The variety stimulates him to create his own way of working, and also helps those who have no ideas of their own.

Many times, the point must be emphasized that originality is more to be desired than technical perfection, and that copying hampers creative expression. The child must believe that his own ideas, developed in his own way, are important and distinctly worthwhile. By adult recognition of his efforts, confidence in his ability to create is strengthened, and his interest in developing his own powers of expression increased. As a result, he will draw more readily, attempt new methods, and find fresh approaches and ways of working.

As the child matures, a consciousness of background and space environment becomes more evident, while a definite awareness of color relations begins to develop. Group work especially is necessary, since the child must feel the need for cooperation and interaction, and that his own contribution to others is important. He learns to share his own knowledge, to be tolerant, and to respect the rights of others. He enjoys working cooperatively with them in carrying out one purpose and in contributing socially to the group. Living and thinking and learning together are necessary for training the child in a democratic society.

Through all the grades, there should be satisfactory growth in appreciation and capacity for design and ease in expression. Art experiences should be continuous; and teachers in each successive grade should follow the best methods of stimulation and guidance to assure the child of steady progress.

In the upper elementary grades, the relation of color to mood begins to be realized, and design is now used consciously as decoration. Three-dimensional form becomes important to the child only when he develops the need; and then merely the simplest forms should be explained. Railroad ties and telegraph poles are examples easiest to be seen and understood.

The older children like to draw from

"THE CITY MARKET"—Subjects of commerce and industry are of interest to the boys.
Lillian D. Olson, Art Teacher, Superior, Wisconsin

models, and they enjoy portraying amusing incidents. Boys from the third grade upward want action, and their favorite creative drawings center around dog-fights in the air or gangster battles on the ground. Thrilling tales of the West, with Indian skirmishes, stagecoach holdups, and buffalo hunts may be integrated with art education to reproduce dramatic history, especially if the teacher will channel it into a personal angle by asking, "What would you have done in that situation?"

Older children are interested in crowds at ball games and on street corners. They like to draw people of other countries. "The Neighbors" never fail to furnish interesting subject matter for illustration. "Over the Back Fence," "Gossip," "A Tea Party" are subjects

Art Expression In The Upper Elementary Grades

that children find familiar and congenial.

They are concerned with the circus, church gatherings, and meetings of all kinds. They like personal and environmental problems rather than English castles and Vikings and portions of history that are unfamiliar to them. Seeing, thinking, and dramatizing make vivid impressions; therefore, familiar things are more vital to them than what they cannot visualize. Unless these vague impressions can be made vivid through reading and television, illustration will be stilted and copied. However, experiences must not be limited to immediate interests, especially with older children.

37

Creative Expression with Crayons

New and unique approaches should be encouraged, and original ideas and viewpoints developed.

Class discussion, both preceding and following a lesson, is invaluable for the exchange of ideas; and personal evaluation helps the child to realize his needs, determine what he wants to say, and teaches him what ends he must attain in order to grow aesthetically. The teacher gives the type of guidance suitable to the particular child, helps him to visualize his experiences, and crystallize his ideas through graphic expression.

Upper grade children should become conscious of what constitutes good design. No formal lessons are necessary, but attention should be directed to it when used in expressing vital experiences or in making craft articles. A feeling for the meaning and use of different types of lines, the understanding of overlapping objects to give a feeling of depth, and the difference in representation and emotion as expressed through pictures to achieve consistent emotional effects should be understood. As skill and mentality develop, an awareness of good design will evolve.

There should be unity in a composition—the whole should be harmonious and satisfying. The center of interest should be emphasized, with dominant lines leading to it. Balance and harmony are achieved through filling the paper pleasingly, and by rhythmic repetition of color, lines, and masses such as rows of houses and people. Line direction, shown by blowing trees and slanting rain, must have opposing lines or counter-thrust to re-establish the balance. The sky areas should appear as an important part of the picture; and there should be variety of shapes and colors, contrast through light and shade, and pleasing textures. Non-objective and abstract design should also have a place in the elementary art program of today.

A decorative mural in broadstroke rendering.
Grade Eleven, Central High School, Oklahoma City

Planning
The Art Program
For Children

THE program of art education should be carefully planned so that each individual may progress according to his abilities, potentialities, and needs. It should attempt to develop the child mentally, socially, and emotionally to help him become an active and contributing member of his social group. It should provide democratic training for all children and educate them in appreciation and a desire for aesthetic betterment in everyday living.

In planning the art program, the teacher should avoid the type of activity that stresses uniformity to a given method, and emphasizes the artistic product rather than the development of the child's personality. Directed activity inhibits the child and prevents the natural sequential growth and development of practical and aesthetic skills; therefore, there should be no tracing or copying, no use of patterns or coloring of hectographed outlines, no uniformity of methods or evaluation, and no formal or imposed directions which limit the creative ideas of the child.

The program should be flexible in order to make use of individual interests, experiences, and activities as motivation for aesthetic appreciation and expression. It should provide for special attention to the development of skills only when the need is felt and sought by the child. It should include art principles informally in class discussion in such a casual way that the child will absorb them as a natural part of his aesthetic growth and use them as tools in his art expression.

The time allowed for art activity also should be flexible enough to permit work to continue while interest lasts. The young child's span of attention is short and his art periods are easier to regulate than those of older children who do not wish to stop at a critical place in their work. It interrupts their plan of action and train of thought, making it difficult to recapture interest in that subject later. Perhaps a tame squirrel has been brought to school, and the class is interested in its shape, its movements, and its habits. Some may want to show it in imaginary coloring while others may prefer to create a feeling of squirrelness itself. Any interruption in the lesson will tend to break the thought so its real worth will be lost or impeded.

A progressive art program should provide challenging opportunities by which the child may learn through choice and decision in solving his own problems. Skills are the outcome of activity properly motivated and the conscious need for expression. Vital, active interest is the important factor in the success of creative results.

The art program should develop individual differences in personality by encouraging the child to act constructively in initiating a large portion of the subject matter he uses for motivation. He should also have a part in evaluating the results. The program should broaden experiences and develop new interests and ideas. Incidents which make excellent motivation for aesthetic expression are often occurring in class and should

39

be used as springboards for drawing and activity projects.

Children grow in knowledge and self-confidence through exchange of ideas. Discussion before and after a lesson should develop interest, help the child to visualize more clearly, and saturate the mind to spill over into spontaneous expression. Discussion which precedes an activity gives the teacher an opportunity to learn the immediate interests of the children. She should then be on the alert to select and make use of suggestions and throw them back to the class as inspiration for creative art.

A rich program should provide opportunity for excursions suitable to the child's interests and mental capacity, and encourage his reactions through the use of crayons and other art media. It should include subject matter that will challenge his imagination and the urge to create. It should provide opportunity for emotional release that will bring him joy and satisfaction. It should create the desire to use his immediate interests, experiences, and activities as motivation for the development of appreciation and creative expression and cause him to seek wider information and more original ways of expressing his ideas.

The art program should provide the type of subject matter that appeals to the different personalities. Vital personal experiences furnish the most satisfactory motivation. The fantastic might interest one child; playing with dolls might be the subject uppermost in another's mind. Individuals react differ-

ently to varying stimuli. One sees and another feels. One child might record the action and excitement of an Indian raid; another might show the ruin left, the grief of a lone survivor, or even place himself in the role of participant.

Somewhere in the program should be a place for democratic group participation to help the child make social adjustments. It should develop cooperation, tolerance, sharing ideas and materials, accepting responsibilities, and acceding to the wishes of others.

To feel that he is a part of the whole creates in the boy or girl a sense of security and a feeling of belonging to his social group.

The ideal program for the elementary schools, therefore, should free the child from prejudices and inhibitions. It should realize satisfying results from integrating art with stimulating experiences and activities of the child, and through choice of subject matter that challenges the imagination and the urge to create. It should release inner emotions to bring joy and satisfaction, increase capacity for appreciation through activity and observations, and encourage a desire for wider information and newer ways of expressing ideas. Art education should be a rich adventure in living. It should bring happiness and spontaneous expression in aesthetic art activity to every child in the grades of the elementary schools.

The Teacher Evaluates The Child's Work

IN ORDER to guide the child to work happily and cooperatively with his contemporaries and make a place for himself as an individual in a social group, the teacher must be able to evaluate his work correctly, and know just what constitutes actual progress in art education.

Most important in successful evaluation of the subject is the attitude of the teacher herself. She must understand the needs of the child to promote growth. She must know that the boy or girl thinks and reacts differently from the adult—that fact and fantasy are not clearly defined in his mind, and that he delights in the impossible as well as the real. She must realize and appreciate the child's viewpoint and his sincerity of expression. She must keep in mind that the development of personality rather than skills or the finished product is the end to be sought, and that child-product, not art-product, is the goal.

Exhibitions of children's work and evaluation by members of the class are important elements in guiding the child to know what is good in art. Certainly he should be aware of his own growth. In comparing his drawings with previous efforts and in seeing the work of others displayed with his own, he will be able to evaluate his own results more correctly and develop an increased sensitivity for art appreciation as well as a feeling of enjoyment in the use of crayons in good color and design.

Praise plays a large part in fostering interest and promoting development, while encouragement all along the way establishes self-confidence and the courage and urge to make plans, and think them through to completion.

In evaluating finished work, the teacher may point out errors only if she offers constructive, friendly help, and gives adequate guidance for improvement. She should phrase her questions to direct thinking and solving the problem at hand. She should not be concerned with realistic proportion or correct draftsmanship. Any criticism which suggests realistic treatment rather than the child's interpretation hampers free expression. Emphasis should be placed upon design and creative expression, on enjoyment and satisfaction and on individual interpretation of the subject and realization of self. Appreciation and encouragement, not criticism, will bring about the desired results.

Aesthetic growth is evidenced in self-confidence and freedom in working. The child should let his imagination romp through his picture, with adventurous characters doing dramatic things. Interest and pride in his work will cause the child to create with freshness of treatment and uniqueness of expression. Vigorous color and ease in applying the crayons, interesting techniques, action, space filling, rhythm, contrast and repetition—the use of these will facilitate and help bring about the development of individual skills and emotional stability.

Creative activity depends upon inspiration either from some outer stimulation or from personal reaction to a vital

Creative Expression with Crayons

experience. The child's drawing should reflect this and give evidence of individual interpretation. It should not be influenced by others, but be uniquely his own. Giving personality and expressiveness to characters he has drawn and evidencing moods and feelings such as happiness and sorrow, loneliness and fear, show thought on the part of the child, and self-realization in his work. When he feels the movement of waves so deeply that the boat in his picture actually seems to rock, he has put life itself into his composition. When the attitude of a bird is so expressive that one can tell what it is thinking, real artistry is born!

With the young child, the expression of many ideas is more important than execution. Much detail also is evidence of active observation and an alert awareness of environment; however, there are other equally important elements in evaluation which follow a period of work.

Did the child enjoy the activity and did he express easily and freely with self-confidence? Did he show thought and originality in using imagery, and evidence a fresh approach in his work and in his choice and treatment of subject matter? Are the colors harmonious and pleasing, and do they express the mood of the picture? Do the colors reflect the child's own reaction to a vital experience? Is there good composition, with a center of interest, and rhythmic lines leading to it? Does the picture express how and what the child really felt? Is the space filled adequately, and are the background areas as interesting as the foreground? Are only essentials used? Are there interesting light and dark arrangements? Does the picture have design quality, with rhythm and movement and dramatic color that show action and art quality and an imaginative, rather than purely naturalistic treatment? Do the colors sparkle, and is the picture alive? Has the child developed a style of his own, and did the art experience help him to project his feelings, and solve the problem sufficiently to bring about emotional growth?

By recognizing these desirable objectives, and by leading the child to widen his interests and increase his ideas, the teacher will help him establish their use as habit, and bring about constant mental and artistic growth. She will encourage the play element and originality of expression. She will know which qualities are of help in building desirable skills and in broadening aesthetic appreciation. She will be able to meet all interests and abilities, and so guide the child that his work will give him the satisfaction of accomplishment and increased power of spontaneous self-expression through art.

Exhibitions of children's work for evaluation by members of the class are an important part of the art program.

Jane Rehnstrand
State Teachers College
Superior, Wisconsin

What is Talent?

To MANY, the words *gifted* and *talented* mean having exceptional skill in representing things realistically in a photographic way. Grownups often wax enthusiastic over the child's accurate reproduction of a buck-toothed rabbit that frequents the funnies, or a mouse that has become a personality through the comics. The parents are sure their child is a prodigy, and they urge him on to do the very thing that will handicap him for real art expression—that is, to copy. The camera reproduces; the artist creates!

When a child signs his name to a copied picture, he is giving himself credit for the work of another. He would not think of copying a story or poem and calling it his own. This should be brought out in discouraging work which is not the result of the child's own thinking.

Art education today teaches that all children can express aesthetically if they are exposed to proper stimulus and environment, and given confidence to develop according to their capacities and needs. Real ability in art lies in the power to express, to create, to design, to originate.

Children vary in their capacity to express. Because of interest, environment, broader opportunities, muscular coordination, and other basic reasons, some are naturally more creative, more alert, more spontaneous than others. They have more original ideas and a finer sensitivity for color, mass, and line. Others may excel in another area of learning, yet find aesthetic expression difficult. These children should be encouraged to develop at their own rate of achievement and contribute what they can to the group.

Pupils with special aptitude for art expression should not be made the center of attention, and pointed out as class artists. This gives them a false pride in their own ability, and causes others to feel a sense of inferiority. Every child should have equal opportunities to develop according to his potentialities. He should be made to feel that he has something distinctly worthwhile to give, and that his contribution to art is appreciated. He should have encouragement in developing his individuality so he will not want to conform to a pattern. His drawings should evidence unique characteristics and methods of work that he personally originates. Fresh use of old ideas, uniqueness of expression, sensitivity to dynamic color combinations and rhythmic design, together with ease in carrying out his plans, as well as ability to visualize form are ends to be attained rather than skill in execution. True art is feeling and thinking art; and it is the mental activity behind the actual drawing that counts. This determines largely whether or not the child possesses exceptional aptitude or so-called talent for art.

Learning To Observe Through Experience

ON EVERY side are exciting things to be seen in all aspects of life—colorful and rhythmic, dramatic in form, interesting in movement. Children should be taught to observe these things consciously and gather visual information in order to have an aesthetic appreciation of the ordinary things around them, be able to recreate their images in graphic form, and develop the ability to recognize whatever is aesthetically correct and suitable to purpose.

For finding and storing up inspirational material, the younger children should take short walks near the school to fill their eyes and see what interesting things they can find in the neighborhood. They should be shown exciting forms and proportions; and they will respond enthusiastically to this visual stimulation. They should note the difference in moods of sunny and cloudy days, look for color and pattern in trees, in clouds, and in all nature forms. They should enjoy design in leaves and the play of light and shade on the ground. They should seek original ideas for art expression, select the unusual, and look for objects worth seeing—the beauty of orange-lined toadstools, and spiderwebs beaded with dew; the grace of a butterfly in flight; formations of frost; the strength of a bridge; the sturdiness of the oak; the color and rhythm of blue smoke; iridescence of oil on pavements; textures of bark.

The older children should take long walks or excursions for more careful observation and information. They should study buildings, interesting contrasts of different materials and satisfying distribution of darks and lights. They should note harmony in simple things that are familiar to them—lampposts and telegraph poles, and people and animals in action. They should not merely see, but try to retain the picture of the object and comprehend its meaning; and then they should attempt to transfer these impressions to paper through crayons.

Children have photographic minds; and if they can be activated to develop this image-forming power, they visualize more clearly and express more accurately. The child stores in memory the particular characteristics of the object and reproduces it surprisingly well. When his interest is aroused sufficiently, he is able to capture such intangible things as the sensation of the flying of birds—the graceful movements, the darting habits of a swallow hunting its food. The teacher should help the child to get a clear mental picture of the object; but the interpretation should be his own.

Seeing a thing, however, is not enough. Actually experiencing an object is very different from sitting in the classroom and trying to visualize it. The sidewalk has a different texture from that of a brick building. It is underfoot and the building towers overhead. The child's experience of the tree is different from the visual reaction of the adult. The child may climb into the branches and feel the bark. He may sit in the tree and look down at the objects below. The boy who drew a circle and called it a tree explained that he was standing under it and looking up. Because he had experienced seeing and feeling, his perspective was his own.

The teacher must be aware of these differences so she may meet them intelligently. The eye level of the small child is opposite the doorknob and as he approaches it, it looks tremendous to him. The part of the cow opposite his vision is the bag, and it naturally forces its image upon him. This perspective of the child, together with actual experience which he uses in his drawing, makes observation plus experience a very live, vital thing. Since the fantastic appeals to children, a method of stimulation that they enjoy is **SEEING FAIRIES.** I tell them that I carry a little fairy around with me—would they like to see it? This excites their interest immediately; and imagination begins to function. I explain that we really do not see fairies with our eyes but with our imagination. That is why grownups cannot see fairies and children can. I hold out my left hand and develop the imaginary image with my right, talking as I do so. I say, "My little fairy is sitting on my hand. If you look closely with your imagination, you will see him. He wears a knitted green suit and a red stocking cap with a little tassel that bobs up and down as he turns his head. He is wearing green pointed slippers that turn up at the toes. Watch him swing his legs! He is looking at you; and he's grinning just as hard as ever he can! How many can see him?" There is always one doubting Thomas who is too literal to use his imagination. But the rest of the class enter into the fun, and soon they are all showing their fairies—tumbling, toe-dancing, perching on one's little finger, or standing on its head. During a visualization of this kind, one boy held out

Learning To Observe Through Experience

his cupped hands and said that the fairy was ashamed of his dirty nails and wouldn't come out; but it had found a blister on his finger and picked it with a pin to let out the water. I recognized this as a personal experience visualized, and was pleased that he had entered so completely into the play.

On asking where fairies lived, I was surprised to get the varied types of answers—in birds' nests, under leaves, in tree-houses. One child said if they lived on the ground, they might get stepped upon, whereon another answered that an imaginary fairy would not mind if it did. Thus critical analysis entered into imaginary thinking.

Another satisfactory method of visualization is the picture-show that isn't there. We look at a spot on the wall where the silver screen might be, and tell what we imagine we see. Everyone tries to create something different, and clearly-visualized pictures are built up from make-believe ideas. This exchange of thought is a powerful stimulus to all the class; and even the most realistically minded children usually respond before the lesson is over.

In preparation for drawing animals, I like to bring in an imaginary lion or bear, or even an elephant for the children to see. First, I ask what animal they would like to see; than I go to the door, and with an imaginary clanking of chains, if the creature warrants such fanfare, the animal—perhaps an elephant—lumbers in. My running comments all the while supply the action for the children to follow.

The old elephant goes through his tricks in his heavy way. One of the children puts a monkey on his back, and

The little boys are fascinated with fire
engines; always popular subjects in lower
grades.

Ella Elizabeth Preston, Director of Art
Davenport, Iowa

A fourth grade drawing which describes an
airplane trip.

Thelma Green, Teacher
Hebron, Ohio

These are the average crayon expressions from an experiment pertaining to observations of children in a one-room school in Douglas County, Wisconsin.

Jane Rehnstrand, Art Consultant

it comes sliding off because the back of an elephant slants, and that is why the natives ride on its head. But the monkey promptly climbs up the elephant's little round tail, and sits triumphantly on its head. Such dramatization makes a vital impression on the child's mind; and after pretending to watch the monkey slide off the elephant's back and knowing the reason, he will always recall that the back of an elephant is not round or flat. If a teacher is able to picture any characteristic dramatically enough, the child will never forget the mental picture that he has formed. Then calling attention to these points in the

47

In the experiment at Douglas County, Wisconsin, small children drew houses, and particularly their own homes.

Jane Rehnstrand, Art Consultant

real animal when it is available, impresses it indelibly on his mind, and he has added it to his mental vocabulary for satisfactory representation when the age of critical awareness develops.

Children love rabbits, and visualization is particularly timely at Easter when I bring in an imaginary bunny that the children did not know was just outside the door. I pretend to stand it on the table and rub its nose with my right forefinger to show the shape of its profile. I outline its long ears and its fluffy tail with all my fingers as I talk. I stroke the outline of its back and call attention to the way its legs bend in different positions. We notice the soft little paws, and the whiskers! The rabbit sits up and begs, bows obligingly, and finally waves goodbye to the class; and the children never fail to wave back to it! And after visualizing animals in this way, realizing the softness of the fur, the gentleness of the pet, we are ready to make drawings of them in any class in

Learning To Observe Through Experience

the school where our visitors from the zoo have been. So children can be made to visualize anything in the world— things with which they are familiar. They do not have to go to the zoo; they do not have to draw too realistically. There is reference material which the teacher can study beforehand to learn the characteristics of any form, and skillfully lead the discussion around to that particular thing.

There are observation lessons to see and enjoy the movements of living animals; and there are always pictures to be had—not for copying, but for learning to see. Then the animal can be drawn in any position the child wishes because he knows how the different parts look and move; and art becomes more meaningful to the child through learning to use his imagination as well as his eyes, and see.

A child of Santurce, Puerto Rico, experiences observation
by making his own visual record of a sailboat.

Emotion

Is Expressed

Through Art

SINCE the senses play a vital part in the development of personality, sense experiences may be used to advantage in stimulating art activity. Recording a sensation rather than an object, and creating an impression is difficult to express. It challenges individual interpretation through art in showing heat, a laugh, fear, happiness, fatigue, excitement, mirth, anger. The emotional reaction must be expressed through color and through types of lines, mass, and texture. The result depends upon the teacher's ability to release creative ideas and make them function.

The child's interests lie close to nature. He likes to listen to the rain on the roof, the sound of the wind. He enjoys the feel of mud oozing through his toes. He captures the essence of his impressions and experiences, and translates them in a direct, forthright, and sincere manner of working. He knows that snow is cold, so he draws it with blue crayon. He interprets the creeping tiger and the stealthy cat with slanting lines. He shows weightiness of the elephant with heavy strokes and dark hues. He pictures the tiny active mouse in yellow, and the slow, dull turtle in unexciting browns.

Making the children aware of texture is best developed through the reaction to touch—the feel of fur, feathers, silk, sandpaper, iron. These sensations may create mental pictures and be expressed

Illustrated here is a graphic emotional record by a fourteen-year-old girl, stimulated by the thought of a lion.

Alma Randolph, West Frankfort, Illinois

50

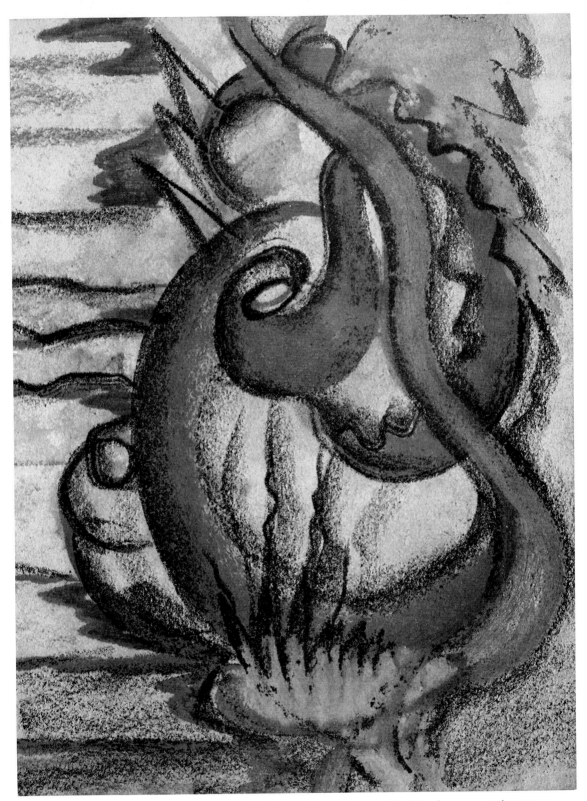

INTERPRETATION OF A MUSICAL THEME—Designs made to music can stimulate the same emotions as hearing the music.

Jane Rehnstrand, State Teachers College, Superior, Wisconsin

51

Creative Expression with Crayons

realistically or in non-objective patterns.

The senses stimulate art activity. Smell may be expressed graphically by the thought of burning leaves, turpentine, wet feathers, cabbage cooking. Hearing may bring about images by thought of a clap of thunder, a baby crying, a siren, a cricket chirping, the buzzing of bees, the mewing of a cat. Taste creates mental pictures through sensations of eating—salt, sugar, pickles, green persimmons; and in all these expressions, the conventional is by-passed, and original thinking encouraged.

In correlation with social science, the oil wells of Texas would carry out the feeling of oil and smoke if drawn in black and browns; and vigorous technique would create the feeling of grime and hard work, while delicate colors and finer treatment would give the impression of a more feminine occupation and type of work.

Different directions of lines contribute to emotional expression. There are horizontal, vertical, curved, and oblique lines. Horses running against rain express action and speed, and restore the balance. Curved lines are graceful and rhythmic, and may be expressed in the billowing folds and scallops of a circus tent, the balloons, and the clowns. Angular lines are reminiscent of the bizarre. Horizontal lines show vastness and loneliness, and vertical lines are uplifting.

Children like to analyze places before drawing them—the desert as a vast area of yellow sand, shown with the horizontal predominating; the jungle with its riot of colors and tangled foliage; and the sea with its calm and rippling waters that seem to move under the tiny curved lines.

An interesting stimulus to emotional analysis is batik paper with spots of color. Grays and mauves might suggest old age; violent contrasts might be interpreted as conflict or anger; and winter, love, contentment, crowds—all might be translated through areas of different hues.

Children should make their own rules for using color, and choose them at will for expression. They like to select the initial hue and find the color it is asking for. They delight in showing mood and feeling in their own way. Genius is rare; but all children can create. When they can draw a tired horse, a gentle dog, a happy child, they have gone far into the subtle meaning of creativity in art.

Children Like To Draw To Music

Music plays a vital part in stimulating emotional activity. Through it, definite feelings are awakened and moods are created to suggest color patterns in artistic form. Through this inspiration, the child listens for what the sound expresses to him—whether the tune is lively or solemn, whether the rhythm glides or jerks, and what the music has to say to him individually. To everyone the MARCH OF THE WOODEN SOLDIERS suggests a tramping sound pattern; the movement of the BARCAROLE brings mental pictures of waves in motion. Other compositions may be more or less subtle in their message to the listener.

Every sound has visual significance and each instrument suggests its particular hue. The rich tones of the organ are like the purple majesty of a cathedral; the dancing notes of the fiddle give the impression of a barn dance in the country, with many colorful hues intermingled. A quiet lullaby might make one think of cool pastel tones; and wild excitement might be expressed in red

DRAWING TO MUSIC

Gertrude Barr, Art Teacher
Congdon School
Duluth, Minnesota

Ruth Maney, Art Supervisor

Work of third and fourth grade
pupils.

*First Stage: Little more than a maze of
lines. Very little attention is given to form*

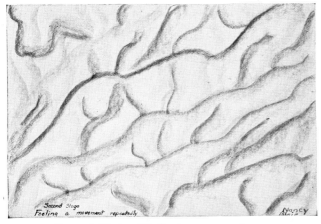

*Second Stage: Distinct movements are
noted in a musical selection*

*Final Stage: Musical selection interpreted
with a definite picture of design in mind*

53

"HALL OF THE MOUNTAIN KING"—A multi-colored wax crayon expression of individual emotion and rhythm drawn from record music.

Lila Hughes Tyler, Lincoln Junior High School, Wyandotte, Michigan

and orange hues. Action is also shown by contrast from a high to a low note, while waltzes give the feeling of a quiet dreamy glide, magnolia blossoms, and dignified pleasure. Classical music would require curves, and zigzag lines would be an expression of jazz.

As interpreted by artists and musicians, each note in music has its corresponding color in art. This is shown by the color organ or clavilux and in radio fountains which produce certain hues when the corresponding notes are played or sung. The sensitive child feels this instinctively and uses color accordingly.

In drawing to music, the pupil should close his eyes and let the rhythm speak to him. Starting with relaxed motions across the paper, he tries to interpret the message the tune has for him. In this way he actually feels the sounds that the music has created in his mind. Colored crayons are an excellent medium for this interpretation as they are at hand when needed.

The loudness or softness of the music suggests the intensity of hue, and the musical theme interprets the pattern of lines, masses, and colors; therefore, color rhythm and design lend themselves most readily to this type of motivation. A dominant color scheme must be accented to set the mood—that is, warm colors such as red or yellow may give the feeling of martial airs. Cool colors set the stage for such feelings as a summer night's dream.

Through the influence of music, texture may be added to the color patterns created by filling areas with circles, dots, dashes, stripes, and wavy lines. Tranquility may be expressed by horizontal lines; action by slanting lines; and upright effects are used for higher aspirations and hopes.

And to the Earth It Gave Great Light

INTERPRETATION OF A CHRISTMAS HYMN

Gertrude Barr, Art Teacher, Congdon School, Duluth, Minnesota

In reverse order, mental pictures create musical themes. There are any number of ideas that may be set to music by the children in one or two lines with emphasis upon the thought and rhythm. If a cat were stalking a bird, what colors, lines, and movements would be used? Suppose soldiers were going to war, and were telling their families good-bye. How might it be expressed, and how may they be shown marching off into the distance?

In interpreting **THE THREE BEARS**, the tramp of the big bear, the crying of the baby bear, and the middle tones of the mother bear might result in interesting color patterns of different tints and shades, textures and hues. Certain colors, in turn, might suggest definite places—the circus, church, a ball game, home. They might bring to mind an orphan, an old man, a beggar, a musician, a clown; or a whole picture might be woven in the mind from looking at the rhythmic pattern and interpreting what it suggests.

Whether one approaches art expression through crayons plus an idea; or through musical notes as the activating force, color and music go hand in hand for the child attuned to the message they hold in store. Music has something definite to say that creates lively interest and vivid pattern through color. Its motivation is through "feeling" rather than visual stimulus, and becomes another avenue of approach to art. Its use brings about increased capacity for appreciation of rhythm, color, and design, and develops broader resources for art experiences of the growing child.

55

OUR HOMES

This mural was made on construction paper, 24 by 36 inches. Fifteen children sketched their homes and arranged them in the "Our Homes" mural.

Adeline Peterson, Teacher, Black River School, Douglas County, Wisconsin

Art Enriches
Other Subjects

WHEN a child draws a mental concept, he sees it before him in graphic form. This enables him to understand his environment more clearly. In like manner, integration clarifies and enriches all subject areas of the curriculum. Thus art makes a unique contribution to the learning process. Music, nature study, social science, language, arts, safety—all become more real and easily understood when coordinated with each other and with art.

When social science is used as motivation, the child must be thoroughly familiar with the subject before he can identify himself as a participant and make his own personal interpretation of the incident with ease and confidence. He understands facts more clearly after he has analyzed them; and other peoples' interests and modes of living become more realistic and intimate when put into graphic form, with the child himself as an actor.

In drawing, children should realize that exact pictures and objects are not to be recreated or copied. Their drawings of historical events frequently show stiff little figures—attempted imitations of those characters shown in the book. The end to be attained is not mere reproduction of the life of a certain community, perhaps with Dutch children padding along the dikes in wooden shoes, or Vikings sailing their ships in fiords; but

art integrated with social science is vitally concerned with present-day activities. The life of the people and their relation to others are the primary objectives.

Recently in a survey of public relations, the children were asked to draw their ideas of a Frenchman. Almost all drew men in French uniforms. A broader and more accurate conception should be given so children will think of other nations as people like themselves.

In order to get a natural interpretation of people of other lands, the children may draw their own interpretation of people at work or play. Then, after they have studied the costume and life of a particular country, they might dress the original people, playing or working in typical clothes. This would not only overcome the mistake of showing an incorrect representation, but it would establish a more friendly relationship toward others when the children realize that they are people like themselves.

Ordinary daily activities provide challenging experiences to motivate creative thinking. The teacher should lead the children to suggest ideas that grow out of commonplace incidents. She should give them opportunity to think, to experiment, and to arrive at their own solutions. The subject matter, after all, is only the springboard for expression of original ideas and methods of work. Interest must first be captured, the problem set through consultation of the teacher and class, and definite satisfaction felt in bringing it to conclusion. FUN IN THE JUNGLE would be an intriguing subject to upper grade boys and girls who are interested in the study of tropical life.

In all integration, emphasis is focused upon imagination and creative expression. Art principles as such are not

Nature and science studies are enriched by the integration of crayon methods of illustration. A colored chalk mural by third graders.

Myrtle Sell, Supervisor; Lydia Balch, Teacher; Albert Lea, Minnesota

Social studies become alive when paper and crayons integrate with the subject of Indians.

Ruth Moore, Teacher; Anna Dunser, Art Supervisor
Third Grade, Sutton School, Maplewood, Missouri

Colorful crayon designs help to illustrate and make notebooks more attractive for all the subjects in the curriculum

Maud T. Hartness, Tampa, Florida

taught; but suggestions may be made from time to time incidentally and brought out in class discussion to carry out the points that make for better appreciation of art.

Such established periods as Fire Prevention Week, Good Book Week, etc., tend to set aside responsibility for the rest of the year. The time to stress accident or fire prevention is any occasion when a catastrophe has occurred, and the children are conscious of the need for special care in preventing accidents or

In studying about people of other lands, the graphic representation so vital to recording the child's mental concepts is easily attained with colored crayons or chalks.

Alvina Barthel, Teacher
Jefferson School, Davenport, Iowa

Creative Expression with Crayons

fires. Special weeks then have more meaning to the children.

Drawings of danger and excitement should show action, and posters should be helpful, such as showing ways of preventing fires. They need not be works of art, but simple, childish drawings that serve to impress the pupil with the reason for care. It is the idea itself, and not the skill shown, that should be stressed. Book Week may devote time to beauti-

times of war. Even the younger children can understand a yellow butterfly on a yellow flower, and remember it as protective coloring.

South America and Hawaii offer many wonderful and exciting approaches to art expression, and typical pictures of the country should be a riot of life and color. Big butterflies and exotic birds help to carry out the theme of the warm climate and its jungle life. Gorgeous designs for textiles can be originated by older children who respond to the un-

A second grade frieze of Noah's animals and the Ark.
Mrs. Juliette Maxwell, Art Teacher, Spring Street School, Atlanta, Georgia

fully illustrated books, and construction work in making portfolios and telephone book covers, bound books and jackets as gifts for others. Farm booklets in the lower grades, with chicks and ducks parading proudly on the cover, might motivate the reading lesson for the day, and add particular interest because of the illustrations.

Camouflage appeals to all children when it appears as a new interest. Older children like to find examples of camouflage in the woods, and draw camouflaged vessels and housetops for use in

limited variety of hue and movement. A study of Rousseau's Jungle would be timely in showing interesting pattern and design. Large decorative panels of South American life would add greatly to the attractiveness of the classroom and to the halls. In integration, there is no limit to what imagination can do in the way of tying up an ordinary subject or area with illustration, color, and rhythmic design.

In integrating art with other subjects, the religious themes should not be neglected. A visit to neighborhood

The attractiveness of colored crayons can stimulate and record a child's early knowledge of space division, thus integrating arithmetic; design planning as needed in art; and repetition, thereby developing a feeling for rhythm.

Hawaiian grade children's crayon drawings show the use of familiar landscapes and motifs.

Mrs. James McLean, Teacher, Waimanalo, Oahu

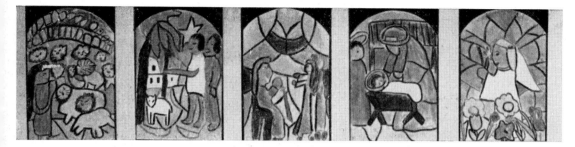

BIBLE STORIES IN CRAYON—Second graders' illustrations of Bible stories.
Mrs. Juliette Maxwell, Spring Street School, Atlanta, Georgia

churches will be full of experiences which they may have had and enjoyed there.

Thus, through integration, every activity in the day may be made more delightful to the child. The meaning of each is clarified, and rich material is always at hand for more aesthetic understanding and appreciation of the world through art.

"A BUSY CORNER"—Water color and crayon study by a sixteen-year-old.
Northern High School, Detroit, Michigan

A social studies mural by the fourth grade—drawn on muslin with wax crayon.

Thelma Lou Riggert, Teacher
Waterloo, Iowa

Sixth grade figure drawing integrated with physical education.

Helen McInnis, Teacher
Gretchen Wahl, Supervisor
Chisholm, Minnesota

The study of community life is enriched by crayon illustrations of its helpers.

Madge Gibbons, Teacher
Second Grade, Tulsa, Oklahoma

Crayon landscape by a fifth grade student.

Julia McArthur, Art Supervisor, Superior, Wisconsin

Outdoor Sketching Involves Interpretation

OUTDOOR sketching is of invaluable help in using different methods of working, and in releasing the creative urge. It illustrates in a concrete way the need for selection of interesting shapes, movements, and colors that make for good composition; it demonstrates the value of creating rather than reproducing photographically whatever is used for inspiration; it helps to develop clearer aesthetic appreciation and an understanding of the picturesque in nature.

Since crayons and paper are so easily carried on a sketching trip, they make an ideal medium for use. The different colors give variety of hue, and the large unwrapped sticks are suitable for quick mass drawing with a minimum of detail.

There should be a definite need in approaching a lesson in outdoor sketching—the drawing of a landscape to analyze the growth and colors in trees; the development of an awareness of beauty in clouds and sunsets; the ability to appreciate the color of birds and to understand their economic value; the increase of knowledge necessary to enjoy design in nature, and the discrimination to select the elements of a good composition.

In order to use these ideas consciously, the child must first have opportunity to get acquainted with what constitutes good design and composition. His attention must be called to these things in the drawings of the class as they occur. He must study them in the works of others who have mastered them. Good pictures by well-known artists will do much to help the child to meet the problems which he must continually face.

In drawing from nature, the child should try not to reproduce what he sees in a realistic way. He should inter-

A nine-year-old's interpretation of an outdoor scene.
Highland, Wisconsin

For the ten- to twelve-year-old who wants his pictures more real, gradation of shading will help to accent the forms within his picture.

Anna Dunser, Sixth Grade, Maplewood, Missouri

Grade children's crayon drawings of trees.

Helen C. Marshall, Art Supervisor, Ironwood, Michigan

Tree drawings arranged to show the progressive development at different age levels. The last two are from junior high school.

Douglas County Schools, Wisconsin

Creative Expression with Crayons

pret and create, not copy. He is privileged to take away or add whatever is necessary to produce a particular impression. He should work for design and composition, catch the mood of the picture before him, and let the result be his personal reaction to what he sees. His own interpretation will bring about an entirely original approach and result.

Trees, themselves, have a definite personality that may be brought out in drawing—the strength and protection of the oak, the grace of the willow, the uplifted feeling produced when one looks at the California redwood.

Before attempting a sketching lesson, the teacher should create an awareness of what the class is going to seek and find. Since nature is not to be copied realistically, the child's ingenuity is challenged to look for things out of the ordinary; or, if it is uninteresting in it-

self, to give it that particular something that would make it unique. By selecting the one outstanding object or quality that the child finds interesting, using only necessary details in stressing color and design, or in developing an idea interesting in its content, and adding a simple background that will emphasize the objects in the foreground, the original treatment given it will serve to set it apart.

This actual striving for something definite will help to develop the ability of the child to create in an original way. He may add a squirrel peeping from the branches of the tree; a hole in the trunk for a woodpecker's nest, or there may be shown an interesting family of birds resting on a limb.

For making decisions of what is to be used in a picture, outdoor sketching offers an unlimited field, and provides just enough subject matter to serve as a basis for creative imagination.

Unusual action has been observed in this drawing by a young student of Douglas County Schools, Wisconsin.

TEXAS BILL OUT RIDING

Cartoons Challenge Humor!

THE drawing of cartoons offers excellent opportunity to develop originality, humor, and inventiveness.

Nearly all children in the upper elementary grades like to draw cartoons, but the project makes the strongest appeal to boys. The girls adapt cartoon drawing to their own interests, and produce many delightful and refreshing creations.

Ideas must have a simple, direct humor and little detail. One of the most interesting and intriguing subjects for girls as well as boys is animals— with people, birds, fish, and pets running a close second. The cartoon showing animals in action has a strong appeal through its element of humor. Snappy sayings and original titles inspire quick thinking. When the boy who drew a mouse swinging on the cat's tail was asked what the mouse was saying, he answered, "May I tail along?" Another suggestion for a single cartoon might be a seal struggling into a suit too small for him and saying to his mate, "I know it isn't a perfect fit, my dear, but I forgot it was woolen when I took my swim."

The one-picture cartoon as an initial project might be an introduction to a series of comic strips such as are popular with young people through the funnies. A character should be original and have at least one personal characteristic to identify it always. The single picture adapts itself to a shorter period of time than the series, and creates immediate interest in itself instead of depending

Cartoons developed from geometric forms in an eighth grade arithmetic experiment.

Mary Casey, Teacher, Waukegan, Illinois

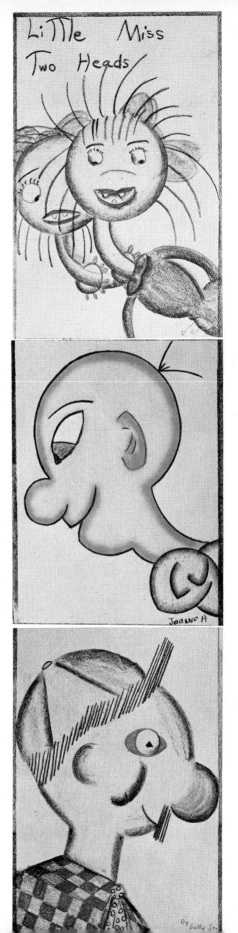

Creative Expression with Crayons

upon suspense. Thus, language might be integrated with art expression.

Clever cartoons of one picture are often found in newspapers and magazines. A number of these displayed on the bulletin board would demonstrate the idea in order to stimulate the children to create delightful and witty cartoons of their own.

Similar to the cartoon is the progressive story in which each child selects a different sentence of a series that contain picture ideas. The children write the story, and interest in illustrating it is a natural result. The story should be simple. "May and Tom went out to play. The sun was shining, and the flowers were blooming. A big white rabbit came hopping up. He showed them where a whole nest of Easter eggs were hidden. Then he hopped away." What happened next is a follow-up of the need to supply the whole class with a picture sentence in each unit of the story.

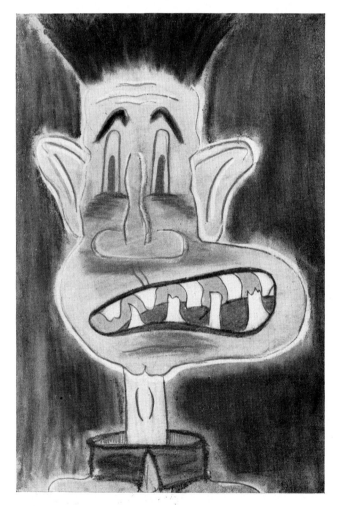

For certain types of boys at junior high school level, the drawing of imaginatively ugly faces seems to be a good emotional outlet.

Virginia O'Leary, Teacher
St. Louis, Missouri

70

Cartoons may be used effectively to impress the rules of safety, cleanliness and other lessons of like kind. A popular type of cartoon suitable for children of the seventh grade is through original poems, stories, or articles written for Safety Week. The child creates the story by selecting the details that help it to move forward, with emphasis upon the idea to be impressed. Then he draws pictures that contain the outline of the story. This is similar to the comic books.

For a cartoon on Safety, Mrs. Bird starts out to market and Mr. Bird tells her to be careful. She collects worms in the middle of the street. A car knocks the basket off her arm and scatters the worms. She flies home and snuggles against Mr. Bird, while the young ones peck at the one worm hanging from the empty basket.

For a cartoon on Courtesy, Mrs. Bird goes marketing for worms. The butcher

Cartoons Challenge Humor!

is a cat. It is raining and he helps her home. Suspense is held in what the cat will do, and the end is a complete surprise when the cat bows gallantly at the nest and leaves.

Similar to the cartoon is the poster as the younger children know it. A work of artistic perfection is not to be desired. The idea is the thing to be impressed and the simple picture with few details and dynamic thought with the right illustration to force it home is the goal. Like the cartoon, wording is condensed, and crayon drawings using colors that carry at a distance and bring home the message so the child will remember it is the function of the poster in the elementary grades. The cartoon is too worthy a subject to be neglected as motivation for witty and delightful expressions of children in creative art.

High school level cartoon faces inspired by Halloween.
John Gilbert Wilkins, Skokie, Illinois

Methods
of Stimulation

THE classroom teacher who has little or no training in art and is just starting upon her career is in need of correct methods of guiding and stimulating the child for creative expression. Subjects such as music and arithmetic have notes to be recognized and tables to be learned, but art is creative. It is an aesthetic experience, and creativity is so intangible that it is difficult to explain just how the source is reached. It requires a teacher with interest and enthusiasm; it depends upon her ability to release the creative urge and to inspire the children to express freely with satisfaction to themselves.

Grade teachers frequently ask, "How can I teach children to draw when I don't know how myself?" In answer to this, one must keep in mind that she is not expected to teach professional art. It is not a matter of drilling as she thinks of it. She must stimulate and guide and inspire. The child learns through activities that engage the intellect and feeling. By reliving his vital experiences and expressing his interests through drawing, his mental and graphic powers develop and he grows in aesthetic ability.

When the child realizes his need of help and asks for it, the teacher must provide the type of assistance that will aid him to crystallize his ideas. She stimulates him to solve his problems for himself. He is so full of interesting subject material ready to be tapped that it may only require stimulation to bring it

out, and encouragement to look with pride on what he has already done. Teaching should find and contribute to the child's needs and simplify his experiences for him.

There are countless ways to stimulate creatively; a sympathetic teacher can lead the class to visualize and create freely through her own methods of approach. When the child is assured that his drawings need not conform to adult standards or be subjected to adverse criticism, he will express joyously in his own way. He will feel free to use whatever color he likes, and he will choose automatically those hues which seem to fit best the mood of his picture. He will sense for himself the need of strong contrast when he finds that his figures do not stand out sufficiently against the background. He will delight in using textures that enrich his expressions and he may add intriguing dots and scallops to the body of an otherwise drab turkey with an abandon that an adult of the old school could not possibly attain.

Two things are vital to creative expression in art—freedom to create and interest. The child must believe in his own ability to start and finish whatever he has in mind; the teacher must provide ample opportunity for individual and group experiences that lead to creative activity. She must furnish a sympathetic environment in which to work and guide the children to enjoy stimulating experiences that challenge initiative and appeal to the imagination of youth. She must know how to liberate the inhibited child and help him clarify his ideas. She must be able to meet the individual needs, instill democratic attitudes, and develop genuine appreciations that will carry over into life situations of different types of children.

72

The farm scene offers stimulating subject matter for individual creative interpretation at all levels.
Ruth Moline and Lydia Jasa, Teachers, Douglas County, Wisconsin

73

Fanciful houses are an inspirational subject for upper grade levels.

Nell F. Shepard, Phoenix, Arizona

Stories are good stimulation for creative drawing. A seventh grade illustration.

Nina E. Krueger, Milwaukee, Wisconsin

"THE CIRCUS WAGON"—The circus is a very stimulating subject for children in the lower grades.
Inez Quall, Teacher, First Grade, Albert Lea, Minnesota

Art activities must originate as far as possible with the child and follow his interests and abilities. For this reason there can be no graduated lessons planned to bring about artistic growth, no prescribed methods of instruction given, and no definite directions outlined to meet every situation. Art should be the result of spontaneous activity.

Interest must be aroused before actual drawing begins. Telling the pupil to make anything he pleases lacks motivation, and interest is not aroused. On the other hand, overemphasis upon skills inhibits the child and hinders creativity. His inspiration comes as the result of a vivid impression, real or imagined; he is activated for creative work through new and exciting experiences and fascinating ideas so he will want to express his own particular reaction to them.

Every art activity should spring from the needs and desires of the class; therefore the teacher cannot know what direction the children's interests will take. She cannot be sure of a predetermined subject or definite method of procedure. If the lesson is so planned that the end is foreseen, the work will not be child-sponsored and it will be lacking in freshness and spontaneity.

During a day at school, a cat might wander in or a bird might sing outside a classroom window. It may happen that a giant mushroom has intrigued a group of children on the way to school, and they have brought it in for the others to enjoy. Mushrooms may suggest the idea of fairies, and the children's interest is readily captured. They might draw their own interpretation of fairies and where they live, how they look, and how they play. Mushrooms may also suggest the woods and the gathering of nuts in autumn. Discussion may turn in any direction and lead to a talk on hiber-

nating animals. Wise selection of these art ideas and use of interesting art models chosen by the children themselves help to sensitize them to designs in nature and bring about an awareness of their beauty—the markings of snakes and insects, patterns and colors in fish, textures and growth of coral. Children have decided preferences in choice of subject matter, and the use of color causes definite reactions in each individual, so it is vital that the child be allowed to make his own decisions and to express as he likes.

Creative art is thinking art. The teacher looks for the child's own interpretation and rendition of the subject; through stimulation and guidance, aesthetic understanding is achieved.

It is important that the real purpose of art education be kept constantly in mind by the teacher—not to produce artists or to make finished articles for show, but to develop the child to his fullest potentialities. Beautiful craft pieces and attractive drawings are always delightful, provided they are the result of the child's initiative and effort. He should produce the best of which he is capable, if it is not at the expense of his personal development.

In order to share ideas and stimulate thinking, every art lesson should be preceded by class discussion in which both the teacher and the children take part. A farm scene might be a subject. Naming a number of animals suggests a variety of choice and opens new channels of thought. This preliminary discussion enables the less creative child to broaden his ideas and originate more freely for himself.

If a particular interest has presented itself as motivation for art activity, the

Creative Expression with Crayons

children may discuss the general theme and make their own decisions of the ideas they would like to draw. When nothing has been suggested, skillful questioning may initiate thinking, perhaps by asking, "What would you like to talk about today? Animals? Let's name some. Yes, pigs *are* interesting. What is your pig doing? Where is it? What particular interest can you give it in your drawing? What colors will tell the story best, or help to supply the proper setting?"

Again, to start an idea when none has presented itself naturally, the teacher may ask, "What did you see on the way to school?" Usually one sees very little of particular interest and there is no response; so the teacher may say, "What would you like to have seen?" If no exciting suggestion is yet forthcoming, she might remark, "I'd like to have seen two little rabbits walking hand in hand to school—rabbit school, each with her satchel, and each carrying her lunch. And, oh yes, I did see a whole flock of robins going north and stopping to eat on the school grounds." Or if she wishes to initiate a more exotic idea, she might say, "I'd like to have seen a boy riding to school on an elephant. It would be fun to have seen a whole parade of elephants, wouldn't it?" Further suggestions from the children help to put over the idea, and imagination brings out all sorts of original and fantastic pictures.

Children are primarily interested in people and how they act. "What hap-

pened to —? What hairbreadth escapes did he have? What was his most embarrassing moment?" Perhaps some might wish to draw a picture in one predominating color to create a particular impression—blue for a cool, icy Eskimo scene; red for danger; yellow for happiness.

With always a wealth of material for motivation, the teacher must be ever on the alert in leading the class to select suitable subject matter for interpretation. Through skillful guidance, she draws out suggestions that are of interest to all— pets, holiday celebrations, home activities, adventure. She encourages the children to supplement these ideas with others as varied as possible and to express them in new and original ways. She leads the children to discard commonplace ideas and let imagination have full play. She inspires confidence to use imaginary themes and daring colors so the result will be vibrant and sparkling. She activates them to look for rhythmic lines, for movement, action, and mood. She tries to cultivate in them a sense of design and a feeling for humor. She praises loose, free strokes and spontaneous expression, and whatever art quality that is aesthetically good.

Seeing through the eyes of others offers an interesting approach to creative expression. Older children would be intrigued by drawing what a migrating bird could see, how an airplane traveler might view the earth pattern below; what one might see if he were nearly blind; what a spider would vision; how a rabbit would be impressed by his surroundings. The natural reaction of a particular person or animal to environment would influence the treatment of the subject matter and would necessitate the child's putting himself in its place and feeling with it.

Another type of imaginative happening results in **FUN PICTURES**. These are particularly provocative and interesting. The child tries to visualize certain impossible happenings, such as a bear rowing a boat or a kangaroo pushing a baby carriage. Children like the absurd, and readily join in the fun. To start ideas humming, the teacher might suggest one or more impossible things and then invite the class to give others. After several ideas have been suggested to get all minds attuned, the children are told to draw something that has not yet been mentioned, to see how very original they can be. If this does not stimulate slow minds to function and originality to blossom, nothing will.

Naming a picture, either before or after drawing, helps to clarify its meaning and also adds to the interest. It is just another way of stimulating the imagination and tends to add dignity to otherwise mediocre work. The title should not be commonplace but it should be unusual enough to attract attention. **THE MOUNTAIN** does not stir any particular interest; **SUNRISE ON THE JUNK PILE** or **ROMANCE OF A DEEP SEA WHALE**, as originated by seventh grade boys might excite even the child with little or no imagination whatever to think and express likewise.

Methods of Stimulation

Before actual work has begun on a lesson, a suggestion may be made to use at least one art experience that has been previously discussed, such as filling the paper, showing action, using line and color to express a specific feeling, adding humor or a unique touch. This will help to make that experience a part of the child's working vocabulary and habits of expression. At times, other experiences may be suggested by the children themselves. A list from which to select for class participation may be written on the board or an arbitrary choice made by the children individually. By spreading this teaching over a space of time and bringing good techniques in as worthwhile assets for drawings that will be exhibited, the ideas will not be taxing but be gradually absorbed as things to recall and use for a higher type of work.

The question is often asked by the grade teacher, "How can the children be guided to make large drawings that fill the paper?" Although this presents a problem to many, it is really a simple matter. Perhaps the children have brought a turtle to school and the class has noticed its feet with its sharp claws and its slow, crawling movements. They have examined it carefully and know just how it looks. They are ready to draw it from the memory pictures they have acquired. The teacher might take a crayon or a piece of chalk and draw a large circle on the paper very roughly or hold her hand over the area to suggest how much space the turtle might occupy. She

Creative Expression with Crayons

suggests it be large so it will be the center of interest and dominate the picture. By making a few sketchy marks on the board or on the paper, she may show that the strokes should be quickly applied with ease. She might say, "Make it bright and colorful enough to be seen across the room. Fill the paper and make your picture interesting. Think what you are going to draw before you put it on paper."

From this simple and quick introduction, the children in a fourth grade made some delightful compositions. There were whole families of turtles following their mothers on the sandy beach. One turtle had fallen into the water and another, falling from the rock wall around the pool, was tumbling fast. One was dressed for turtle school with books and lunchbox. The turtles were all large, either shown as a family or as a single unit; and the cool greens brought out the feeling of the water in a pleasing way.

Chickens and ducks and dogs and cats are such familiar things that children are likely to mention them at any time. Discussing ducks with human attributes stimulates visioning them in all sorts of situations—strolling down a busy street, carrying umbrellas in the rain, sporting under the bathroom shower or taking part in the horse races while feathered audiences cheer them on. Grandpapa

"SUPPOSE YOU WERE A DUCK"—Ducks became the delightful motivation for an art period.
Mrs. Juliette Maxwell, Art Teacher, Spring Street School, Atlanta, Georgia

A personified duck deftly drawn in wax crayon by a third grader.
Sault Ste. Marie, Michigan

Drake tucks his hoe under his wing and plants flowers in the garden while he secretly hunts for worms. School-going ducks cross the street under the watchful eye of the traffic officer. Some ducks fish, while others enjoy themselves under the Florida sun.

Interesting subjects such as this cause the children to think of themselves as ducks or what not. They adore paddling in the rain, so it is near their hearts. SUPPOSE YOU WERE A DUCK will always bring a satisfactory response. Moving pictures, television, familiar happenings are experiences to be counted upon for inspiration. Imagination will function as fancy soars. Then color and line, and all the principles of good design fall into place and develop the child and his personality through creative activity,

Holidays Have Modern Approach

ALL special days are exciting events in the lives of children, and they offer interesting incentive for creative art expression.

The use of sentimental motifs such as Christmas wreaths, trees hung with snow, and bells tied with ribbon, done in the naturalistic fashion, are taboo; but these symbols can be brought up to date by revamping the approach and leading the children to create original designs of their own. Christmas bells can be colored in delightfully gay hues and decorated with dots and scallops.

Christmas is such an intriguing time of anticipation that the theme can be used for several weeks before the holidays. Young people delight in making gifts for the family—scarfs and table mats and doilies—decorated with wax crayons and pressed with a hot iron to make the colors fast in washing. Then there is paper to be designed for wrappings; there are boxes to be decorated for holding gifts; and there are ornaments to be made for the tree. Gaily dressed dolls, colored with crayons on brown wrapping paper, stuffed, and button-holed around the edges make cuddly toys for little invalids; immense Christmas cards, decorated with appropriate motifs or with drawings of Christmas morning, trimming the tree, and other family activities of the season are attractive additions to the classroom walls, and pleasing to children of all ages since it is of their own creating.

Turkeys and Pilgrims still sport through all Thanksgiving art; but the time-worn turkeys standing beside the proverbial pumpkin, and processions of Puritans filing to worship are no more. Instead of the conventional Puritan, the child's self-portrait in the typical costume of the early settlers of Massachusetts would have a far greater appeal to the modern child if the coloring and general contour at least is like the person drawing it. Another thought-provoking approach would be the portraiture of a Puritan with the age, the distinguishing features, and even the character of the person brought out through the crayons. Naming a figure also would give it personality and call to mind that there were others than Priscilla and John Alden in the group.

Nowadays, Thanksgiving turkeys may wear stripes and scallops with multicolored feathers designed according to

Halloween inspirations became a good introduction to design.

Third Grade, Tulsa, Oklahoma

Thanksgiving inspires many versions of the turkey.
Mrs. Juliette Maxwell, Art Teacher, Spring Street School, Atlanta, Georgia

Wax crayon is an easy medium for holiday characterizations.
Mrs. Juliette Maxwell, Art Teacher
Spring Street School, Atlanta, Georgia

the child's whim. This offers a more glamorous approach. Large fruit in fanciful colors, designed and cut out, add to the interest of the classroom if pasted together in long swags to hang on each side of the windows. The placing together of the fruit by the children themselves would give opportunity for color combination and arrangement, and with the less attractive pieces tucked behind the better-looking ones, it should make a most creditable display, with everyone in the class having a part.

Halloween perhaps offers more thrills and delightful horrors than any of the special days. There is something about a black cat that sends shivers up and down one's spine. At the same time, enough humor is involved in making Halloween masks and creating ludicrous situations that it becomes a fasci-

81

Creative Expression with Crayons

nating project. The startling effect of orange and black—emblematic of the fulfillment of the harvest followed by death and decay, helps to produce an exciting reaction. Grinning pumpkins may still delight the younger children, but they no longer intrigue the older pupils who need more unusual presentation. The conventional Halloween bats and witches are not stimulating to creativity; but weird colors that are suggestive of witchcraft and the spirit of the season, rather than the mere symbols, should be re-created on paper. Drawing to music is particularly good at this season. Rhythmic patterns of a different type are brought out through crayons by listening

to the "Danse Macabre." "The Dance of the Goblins" and others such as the "Witches' Dance" by McDowell are always inspiring as creative stimuli. Another departure from the conventional is the drawing of Halloween heads with distorted features that produce a feeling of the bizarre, with pointed noses, oddly shaped teeth, and wildly flowing hair.

Emphasis on coloring with crayons produces unusual effects—a man with normal features, but whose hue is a weird lime-green; a lemon-colored lady with red eyes and vivid green hair, posed against a purple background; a chartreuse gentleman with bristling, blue hair against a deep red background; or a cross-eyed boy with large, flapping ears and buck teeth, together

"The First Christmas"—by a first grade student.   *Anna Dunser, Maplewood, Missouri*

The freedom of wax crayon used in various textures gives opportunity for individuality in freehand, multiple production of program covers. *Anna Dunser, Maplewood, Missouri*

with enormous freckles—with black cats scattered helter-skelter over the background.

Cats and witches will elbow their way into Halloween. Children's original drawings of black cats in all positions and sizes might be cut out for a delightful border around the room. Cats and other Halloween symbols drawn against a vivid background, and cut up as jigsaw puzzles make purposeful occupational seatwork for rainy days.

The younger children like to draw flat masks of unusual characters to wear. Crayons applied brightly lend themselves well to this work. Older children might integrate the study of African masks with the activity, rendering them in brown and white design somewhat like the originals. No. 16 paper bags, slipped upside down over the head so the eyes, nose, and mouth can be marked personally and cut out after coloring is done, are attractive. Hair, nose, and ears are added, and grotesque colors used. An owl might be dressed in a red cape and witch hat in decorative style, and mounted on a startling color. Scarecrows, bats and pumpkins somehow belong to Halloween, and can still be used with original touches that come only from the imagination of the child sufficiently freed under the skillful guidance of a wise teacher.

Creative Expression with Crayons

Like other holiday projects, the making of valentines should be carefully motivated in order to get purely creative results. Hearts are a frequent choice. These can be decorated with naturalistic or abstract designs. The most attractive idea is the valentine heart designed decoratively in appropriate colors, showing good composition and interesting areas. The important thing is the original slant that is the child's idea in concrete form. Large drawings may show seasonal activities, such as sending or receiving valentines, perhaps with hearts or musical notes or flowers—whatever the child prefers and uses naturally, scattered over the background. The Land of Make-Believe might show crayon drawings of animals shopping for valentines or following any of the season's interests.

Easter brings its parade of people and animals—rabbits in design and chicken book ends, all drawn with crayons. Rabbits may be made into stuffed toys of either cloth or paper, decorated with crayons applied heavily, such as lady rabbits in flowing dresses or sailor bunnies in sea-going attire.

Subjects suggestive of the season stir the imagination to activity. In drawing THE RABBIT'S TEA PARTY, the usual picture would be rabbits seated around a table under a tree. A different approach should be encouraged. Questions such as "Where is it? How do the rabbits look? How do you know it is a tea party?" bring satisfactory results.

To get a new slant on an old idea, illustrate BUNNIES ON PARADE by dressing them in Easter clothes and new bonnets, all going shopping. THE BUNNIES' EGG HUNT, EASTER DANCE AT RABBITVILLE, A RAB-BIT FAMILY AT EASTER, MOTHER BUNNY HIDES THE EGGS, PICNIC IN RABBIT PARK, HAS ON AN EASTER BONNET—these are all subjects that children would like to illustrate. Children will be original in suggesting other titles, and they will be more interested in carrying out ideas which they themselves have suggested.

Rabbit book ends made of wood and colored with crayons, then waxed, would make a worthwhile addition to the reading table. Rabbit dolls drawn and cut out by the children might also be shown in the local newspaper with clothes that children would like for Easter. In this way, they feel that they have had a real part in shaping fashions in a big way.

Of course, Easter would not be Easter without hard-boiled eggs. With designs applied with wax crayons and dipped in a water-soluble crayon bath, they would be an attractive project just before Easter Sunday if done in the classroom of any elementary grade.

Rabbit aprons, cut out by the children and fitted to other children in the class, perhaps designed with the ears forming the shoulder straps, or with crayon decorations appropriate to the season, would be interesting for the children to make. Easter bonnets are always delightful projects with crayon designs forming part of the hats.

On Mothers' Day, children like to take home something practical as well as beautiful—an original picture well mounted on colored background; a self portrait, all wrapped in paper decorated with appropriate motifs. Hearts, turkeys, rabbits, ducklings, spring flowers, a chicken farm—all make interesting designs for allover wrappings.

Seasonal art projects—not something copied or too difficult for the children to undertake with confidence, but a simple activity which is their own and which gives pleasure and satisfaction in creating for a particular occasion or need—that is the art project that should be the natural outcome of holiday occasions that come along as the year rolls on. Such ideas give the children a feeling of freedom in letting their imaginations run wild; the play element exerts a strong influence and appeal in assuring good results at the start. A few suggestions might be made by the teacher to be sure

Holidays Have Modern Approach

the idea is understood—that is, if the thought has come from the class at the beginning. This introduction followed by the remark, "Draw something that no one else has thought about! Let's have something really exciting!" is enough, and the seasonal activities, expressed through the medium of crayons, will take care of themselves.

White or colored crayon lines upon slightly warm boiled eggs produce colorful resist designs when dipped in dyes.

Esther deLemos Morton

Seasonal subjects in many moods are easily captured with wax crayons.

Nell E. Shepard
Phoenix, Arizona

Giving

New Slants

To Old Ideas

*T*HERE is nothing new under the sun; but there are always fresh ways to present the same old ideas to render them fascinating and alive.

The child likes subjects that give an unusual or unexpected twist to imagination. THE RAT THAT SWALLOWED THE CAT appeals to him because of its absurdity, and he will put new enthusiasm into developing fresh ways of expressing himself in order to carry out the idea successfully.

Designing magic flowers in the lower elementary grades appeals to the imagination of the young child, and gets away from the naturalistic. It offers excellent opportunity for creative expression and design. Having no stems, and scattered over the paper, these make delightful pattern designs for decorating textiles.

Hobbies also are intriguing as motivation for art education—snakes, rocks, wild specimens. Sports also are interesting, especially to the boys of the upper grades, while girls like to portray games, home activities, and the things that most closely touch their lives.

Fantasy plays an important part in the young child's life. His is a world of imagination where nothing is impossible. He likes to picture mermaids and mythical creatures at home, at work, at play. The fairies' ball in the forest where the wood nymphs dance, Superman who flies everywhere in space, Easter fantasies with rabbits and woodland creatures sitting on toadstools and playing together—all appeal to the unhampered imagination of the young child.

Youth likes pretense of all kinds, and dramatization renders it more realistic. The girl is a princess with long hair; the boy becomes a pioneer of the old West, and fights Indians with a feeling of being with them in person. He likes to vision the kind of situation he would occupy if he were a turkey at Thanksgiving, a rabbit at Easter, a galloping pony. He sees himself taking a ride in the first auto. The sign FOR SALE holds a story for him. Something exciting might be hiding right now in the grass for him to find. And what about the chick that does not care what the others think of him!

Funny and impossible situations may motivate art expression—anything an animal cannot do, such as pigs climbing trees and elephants in an Easter parade, a bear dancing to the organ-grinder's music, and an alligator riding piggyback. Naming a number of animals with impossible ideas starts the imagination; and then by saying, "Now everybody think of something new and see how funny you can make it," a hilarious lesson results.

"THE EASTER PARADE"—with a child's slant. White chalk and black crayon were used to give a furry effect to the rabbits.

Ann G. Powers, Camarillo, California

Creative Expression with Crayons

There are new vistas to be investigated—how to make snow look soft; the way to show cold; how things look to a butterfly; how the mouse appears to the cat; what one would see in a cave or under a big rock.

Besides drawing insects in design, there are interesting ways of using them in crayon drawings. Imagination must be active, and the insects visualized as people. They might be flying through the air with market baskets. They could be watching a grasshopper boy picking up a cigarette. One might pose as a huge spider with big blue eyes and a red mouth—ideas which the children easily bring to mind.

There might be insects serenading with musical instruments, chewing tobacco, playing baseball, going shopping, watching another on television, skating. Each must be given personality and occupy its own niche in the insect world. Other ideas might be developed such as panels for nature study showing the fanciful in crickets leading their dogs, or on parade. Frogs at school, white mice sliding down the cheese, crickets dancing—whatever the imagination can conjure up in an active mind is material for creative expression.

One of the most interesting ideas developed from the use of insects in drawing resulted from the kind of insect the children would like to be if they themselves were insects. There were crawly worms in red and black fur trimming. There were blue-green dots on the orange body of a potato bug. There were violet bugs with yellow buttercup wings. And when these were drawn very large with the side of the crayon, trimmed with the point to give bright decoration, and cut out, they were most effective in color and design and general interest.

The circus is a form of collective activity with movement in spots, or with one portion of the grounds shown. Activity is felt through many small areas of color. A parade should show movement, with interesting forms rather than mere animals in sequence. A unique idea should be introduced, such as a dog dressed as a monkey, or perched on the head of the lead elephant.

Putting several spots of color on the paper stimulates imagination to creativity. Faces may evolve, with expressions showing emotion, or animals may be the outcome of initial spots of varying shapes and hues.

If well developed, the old-fashioned picture-show is a nice project for all the grades of the elementary school. When this idea was first introduced, children made tiny drawings that could not be seen across the room; and these were pasted to a broomstick inserted in a carton. The reel had to be persuaded to move each time the picture was shown.

To be a success, the drawings should be large with a minimum of detail. The carton itself should be decorated like a theater with appropriate motifs, while the method of making the curtain slide on wires should stimulate thoughtful planning.

The drawings should be attached firmly to a roll of tough paper to move easily on the stick. THE STORY OF A BLACK CAT might be written and illustrated by the children at Halloween, drawing big black cats having dramatic experiences before the story is complete.

Drawing character portraits is intriguing in the upper grades. It is most interesting to see what types the children will select, and how well they show certain characteristics. By distorting some of the features, they secure definite impressions—the hurdy-gurdy man, a tough guy, a beggar, the old woman who sells papers on the corner, the leader of the band.

A short discussion of types that one finds on the street, at home, or in the news should precede the drawing to get the class in tune with the subject and start imagination working. The "fighter" with his rather coarse features, the timid old lady that lives around the corner, the movie actress, the boy with freckles—all have certain characteristics that set them apart from others. The children should think of other people who intrigue them—imaginary characters that come to life under their deft crayons. It is a delightful and mirth-provoking subject to use for an art lesson on a rainy day.

People in general are more interesting to children than any other thing. They

Giving New Slants To Old Ideas

identify themselves with the people they draw, and it is surprising how fresh and delightful these portraits are. The children like to select and suggest their own characters—the man with the big ears, the ugliest character in town, etc.

In drawing portraits, design qualities should be kept in mind. After the features are drawn, certain lines and parts may be exaggerated and spaces filled in to bring the design quality to the drawing. Clowns make excellent subjects on which to start, and related ideas such as balls for the baseball player may add to the background areas. Umbrellas and rain make interesting fillers; and chefs may have bowls and spoons or other kitchen utensils in the picture.

For teaching composition, crayon characters and objects can be colored on paper, cut out, and pasted on outing flannel of the same shape. These can be moved about on a square of flannel which forms the background. Trees, houses, people can be used and moved again and again as often as desired. The drawings backed with flannel will stick to the soft cloth without paste.

So old ideas can be renewed and used with new slants that bring fresh interest and enthusiasm for artistic expression through the medium of crayons—plus imagination set free to function.

Crafts
And Design
Satisfy The
Utilitarian Sense

CHILDREN in the upper elementary grades like to make objects of utilitarian value. They are interested in creating gifts for seasonal activities and for the home. This craftwork furnishes muscular coordination and develops understanding of the product as well as the process involved. It also provides occupation for leisure time, encourages creative ability and initiative, and suggests ideas for original expression.

The wax crayon lends itself particularly well to designing textiles since they can be washed and still hold the color if they have been covered with a damp cloth and pressed with a hot iron.

Even in the kindergarten, children can draw dolls delightfully; and large wall hangings can be made by letting each child draw a figure, and space them over the surface as they wish. If drawn rather large and colored heavily with wax crayon, the idea works up charmingly.

Children like to draw magic flowers, birds, animals, and butterflies; and these are delightful motifs for design if applied to a cloth of pastel hue, or to textiles which the children have dyed solid before decorating.

Older children enjoy designing whole panels of birds, fish, and other specimens in which they are interested. Fish may be given the effect of movement by being drawn at an angle, or by the tails being turned in different directions. Decorative groups of fish, some behind the others, may be colored in brilliant hues with the design quality secured with dots, stripes, and scallops. Related objects of undersea life are used for balance and interest.

Pot holders are favorite craft articles and may be attractively designed, then lined with several thicknesses of huck toweling and sewed together with buttonhole stitch around the edges.

For integration with the study of Mexico, rugs and blankets or serapes showing typical Latin motifs may be designed on cloth with crayons for class plays. Stripes and scallops are quite successful; and these also furnish a colorful decoration for the classroom if used as wall hangings.

Older children especially like to make luncheon mats by fringing pastel colored linen, then decorating them with original designs. Simple drawings such as houses, trees, with people may be quite effective and delightful for luncheon or breakfast sets that resemble old-fashioned samplers.

Wild flowers of the section, birds, people, and leaves may be designed with

A first grader demonstrates how attractive slip covers may be made for library chairs. She drew the design on unbleached muslin and then used the iron to set the colors into the cloth.

Mrs. Atkinson, Teacher; Elizabeth Robertson, Director of Art, Chicago, Illinois

wax crayons on squares of cloth and held together with solid color sewed between the pieces and around the edges for quilts. In this project each child might contribute a square. Studying these specimens for identification in nature research, then using them as recalled and interpreted in worthwhile design is always of interest to the children if the idea originated with and is developed by them.

Children like to decorate their classroom curtains: and half curtains of theatrical gauze decorated with crayoned animals are intriguing to the younger children. Colored notes might be applied for a musical theme, or full-length cream curtains with big white rabbits or ducks outlined with brown or any dark colored crayon, with orange feet and bills, are most delightful for primary grades. These motifs are suggested in order that others may be chosen and designed by the children. Covers for chairbacks can be decorated with animals, flowers, color patterns or any idea that

Outlines for designs on paper-bag masks were made with crayons, and the areas colored with water colors.

Josie di Maggio
New Orleans, Louisiana

Large, gay fairy flower designs were drawn on muslin by kindergartners, making a permanent, indestructible record of their first flower studies.

Toni Cherpes, Teacher, Dimondale, Michigan

"FLOWER CRAYON STENCILS"—With the same stencils, each student produced varied creative flower forms using wax crayon.

Grades two through six, Shirley Polanksy, Rockville Centre, New York

comes to mind. Pieces of cloth a yard square make lovely scarfs if illustrated with children skating around the edges, birds flying, animals running, and other motifs that children enjoy carrying to completion. A continuous picture of outdoor life would be particularly attractive.

A nice project is the designing of handkerchiefs with barnyard scenes or with animals of the zoo. An allover jungle pattern with perhaps a giraffe balanced with palm trees, would be delightful and simple. Clowns, people, toys, soldiers, cows can be made interesting and unique if the child is allowed perfect freedom in creating his own designs. In the same way, larger squares can be designed and made into sofa pillows or cushions.

Young children like to make temporary mats of paper using seasonal activities as motivation, and scalloping the edges or cutting them with pinking shears. When parents are coming to lunch at school with the children, designs drawn directly on paper are always appreciated. These scalloped and outlined with crayons make nice place mats for the luncheon table. Most attractive mats can be made even in the kinder-

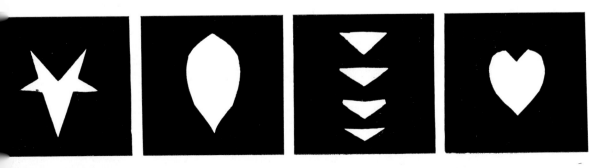

Toy birds, made from natural plywood or coated with white tempera, might have design textures added with wax crayon.

Bernice V. Setzer, Art Supervisor, Des Moines, Iowa

garten with designs, using crayons, on colored poster paper and mounting them on oblong lace doilies. The mothers adore them!

Simple designs may be made by drawing around a coin and overlapping the circles in pleasing ways. "What you might do with a penny" might be an appropriate theme.

Designing a square to protect the table from flower bowls, covering it with glass, and binding the edges with a strip of ordinary gummed tape to hold the edges together is an interesting and useful project. A piece of felt under the square gives it a nice finish.

Little children often cover papers with areas of different colored crayons applied in spots and blended or showing contrast. This is the result of pure enjoyment in applying color.

Puppetry experience for the early grades is easily satisfied with cut paper, wax crayon, and discarded boxes.

Frances Pensyl
Third Grade, Westfield, New Jersey

FROM CRAYON TO STITCHERY—Wax crayon is the perfect medium for hand-craft design planning in the schoolroom.

Grade Four, Bernice V. Setzer
Director of Art, Des Moines, Iowa

Wax crayon designing on paper plates is an excellent introduction to ceramic design. This semi-craft is adaptable to all levels.

95

The paper plate above was decorated in wax crayon at grade level.
Anna Dunser, Maplewood, Missouri

Portions of the paper showing interesting design may be cut in rectangular shape and made into a folder that is lined with a solid color. The edges are punched and laced together with wool floss threaded through the holes.

Ordinary wrapping or craft paper may be used in numerous ways. Sewed dolls are nice if stuffed with shredded or torn paper and laced together on the edges or sewed with the buttonhole stitch. Larger character dolls may be made by older children, and colored with crayons before stuffing with cotton. Toys of all kinds may be made in the same way, using drawings made by the children as patterns for their toys.

Seat pillows for the floor may be made of large circular or square craft paper

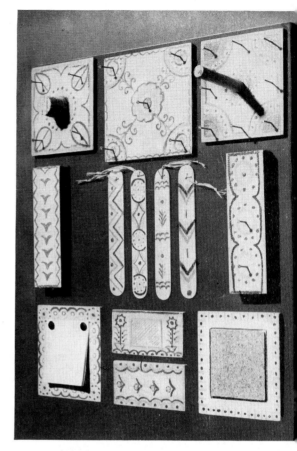

WOODCRAFT DECORATED IN CRAYON—Simple, unfinished wood forms are inviting material for wax crayon decoration.

Julia McArthur, Supervisor of Art
Superior, Wisconsin

Woodcraft Decorated in Crayon

DECORATED PAPER TOWELS—Paper towels, wax crayon decorated, for a Mother's Day project.
Jane Rehnstrand, Superior, Wisconsin

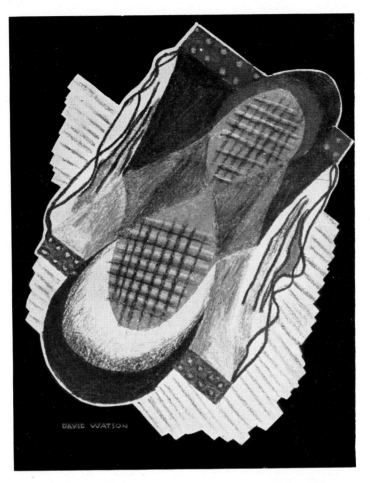

ABSTRACT DESIGNS—Wax crayon techniques are unsurpassed for exploring line, form, and color in early, non-objective design experiments.

Junior high school level, M. B. Mize, Art Teacher
Indianapolis, Indiana

scalloped around the edges and decorated with original designs. These may be sewed or laced together with strips of colored silk, and stuffed with shredded paper.

Two small circles of brown paper, put together with the buttonhole stitch, make a nice cord holder. The end of the cord is threaded through the hole in the center of the floral design or the mouth of a clown, and the ball is held between the two pieces.

Wooden door wedges may be stained with dissolved crayon shavings applied with a cloth or brushed on the wood. Crayon designs are then added with the point of the crayon for enrichment.

In making games, Ring Toss is designed from a circle of cardboard or wood, six inches in diameter, and decorated. A piece of wood cut from the end of a broomstick is nailed upright in the middle of the circle; and rings made of cardboard or small rope are used to toss over it.

97

Creative Expression with Crayons

Throwing the Beanbag is another game composed of two heavy cardboards twelve by eighteen inches, hinged at the top and held steady with tapes near the bottom so they will stand. The front opening may be a clown's mouth, a Halloween pumpkin, a moneybag or a series of circles—something appropriate, planned and designed by the child to outline the hole for the bag to enter when thrown.

The beanbags themselves may be designed in interesting ways, using colored crayons, and pressing with a warm iron to make the color fast.

Blocks may be made of lightweight cardboard and colors applied to the sides. This gives opportunity to cut letters of the alphabet. Jigsaw puzzles with basic ideas such as birds or animal designs may be cut in any number of pieces depending upon the age of child who will use them. These furnish intriguing, creative seatwork for rainy days. The children should originate their own ideas for the composition, and think of other games they can create.

Place cards, favors, bags, greeting cards, blocks, book jackets—all may intrigue the children in using crayons and creating their own original designs for craft articles of utilitarian value.

Creative art is not taught; it is a manner of working, an original expression that evolves from the knowledge one has at his command, and the reaction to experience. It is the spark that lights art education and makes it a developing factor in the life of the child.

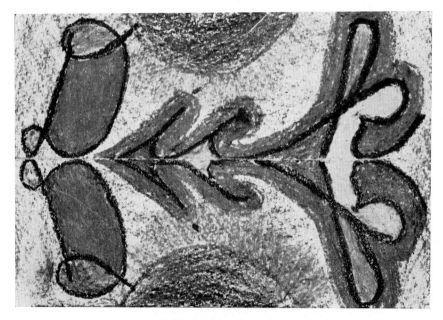

Design stimulation in the grades might be motivated by writing a name on a crease and duplicating it on the opposite fold. The areas become the motif of the design.

Anna Dunser, Maplewood, Missouri

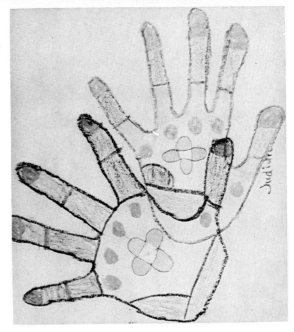

The idea of free form design can be easily grasped by younger students when associated with such familiar shapes as their own hands.

Third-Fourth Grades, Chaille H. Wheelock, Teacher
Benson, Illinois

...tic cut paper forms arranged one on the other and given ...ynamic line of direction with black crayon.

Saturday Classes, Marion Modena, Teacher
California College of Arts and Crafts
Oakland, California

...ometric design is easily explored with wax crayons and ...per folded from corner to corner.

Margaret L. Fiock, Phoenix, Arizona

An always popular method of design, feasible for the lesser creative members of grade classes, is the building up of design forms within the blocks of squared paper.

Anna Dunser, Maplewood, Missouri

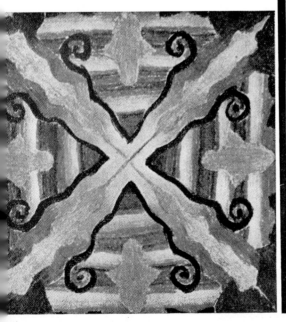

A chalk crayon drawing.
Third Grade, Beatrice Meyer, Teacher
Santa Paula, California

Davis Advertising, Inc., Worcester, Mass., U.S.A.